PRAISE FOR *A LEAGUE OF DANGEROUS WOMEN*

"Mary Frances is one of the most dangerous women I know! She's not afraid to boldly go where many fear to tread—into the lives of broken women who've been sexually and emotionally battered. I recently had the privilege of visiting with Mary and one of Wellspring's beautiful beneficiaries. It was a 'WOW!' moment for me. It is so evident that God is pouring out His lavish love through Mary, quenching many thirsty hearts and revealing Himself as the Living Water that truly satisfies and transforms."

—Shannon Ethridge, MA, bestselling author of the Every Woman's Battle series

"An incredible journey of rescue and restoration! *A League of Dangerous Women* is what the gospel is all about...God meeting us in desperate places, remaking our hearts with stunning acts of love and grace. These amazing stories are tangible proof that nothing is too difficult for Him!"

—Louie Giglio, Passion Conferences, author of *I Am Not But I Know I AM*

"Let your life be blessed as you see for yourself the trophies of God's grace."

—Sheri Rose Shepherd, author of *His Princess: Love Letters from Your King*

"*A League of Dangerous Women* is a collection of incredible stories about women once lost in the mire of life. You will not find despair in the closing chapter of the book, but rather the all-consuming love that only God gives when He intersects a life. You will be inspired by their journey!"

—**Crawford and Karen Loritts**, senior pastor, radio host, and speaker

"In *A League of Dangerous Women* you will meet real women whose lives cry 'Yes!' to Jesus' ability to transform anyone. Be encouraged. The gates of hell cannot stand against the testimony of dangerous women who have experienced God's forgiveness and love."

—**Robert Whitlow**, bestselling author of *The List*

A LEAGUE OF
DANGEROUS
Women

MARY FRANCES BOWLEY
WITH JAMES LUND

Multnomah Books

A LEAGUE OF DANGEROUS WOMEN
published by Multnomah Books
A division of Random House, Inc.

© 2006 by Mary Frances Bowley
International Standard Book Number: 1-59052-800-X

Cover design by Kristin Paul
Cover photo by Steve Gardner, www.shootpw.com
Interior design and typeset by Pamela McGrew

Unless otherwise indicated, Scripture quotations are from:
The Holy Bible, New International Version
© 1973, 1984 by International Bible Society,
used by permission of Zondervan Publishing House
Other Scripture quotations are from:
The Holy Bible, New King James Version (NKJV)
© 1984 by Thomas Nelson, Inc.
Holy Bible, New Living Translation (NLT)
© 1996. Used by permission of Tyndale House Publishers, Inc.
All rights reserved.

Multnomah is a trademark of Multnomah Publishers
and is registered in the U.S. Patent and Trademark Office.
The colophon is a trademark of Multnomah Publishers.

Printed in the United States of America

For information:
MULTNOMAH BOOKS
12265 ORACLE BOULEVARD, SUITE 200 • COLORADO SPRINGS, CO 80921

Library of Congress Cataloging-in-Publication Data
Bowley, Mary Frances.
   A league of dangerous women / by Mary Frances Bowley with James L. Lund.
      p. cm.
   ISBN 1-59052-800-X
   1. Christian converts—Biography. 2. Women in Christianity—Biography.
3. Conversion—Christianity—Case studies. I. Lund, James L. II. Title.
   BV4930.B69 2006
   277.3'0830922—dc22
   [B]

                                                      2006039252

07 08 09 10—10 9 8 7 6 5 4 3 2 1

DEDICATION

To my heavenly Father, who every day takes the dangerous risk of loving His fallen and broken children—including me. You are the reason there is a story to write!

To my husband, Dick. There is no one who could have supported his wife as much as you. You believed in God's work through me and sacrificed so I could follow the Lord. You are the BEST!

To every courageous young woman who walks in the door at Wellspring. I love you all.

A NOTE FROM THE AUTHOR

All of the stories in this book are true. Many of the names, and a few minor details, have been altered to protect the privacy of the people involved.

Profits from sales of *A League of Dangerous Women* will go to further the work of Wellspring Living.

TABLE OF CONTENTS

FOREWORD

Several years ago I sat across a lunch table from Mary Frances Bowley and entreated her to write this book—a book that would allow everyone to experience the miracles she sees every day. If strippers, prostitutes, and heroin addicts can be utterly transformed by the unconditional love of God, anyone can. And once transformation takes hold, the recipient of that new, abundant life becomes utterly dangerous to the power of darkness.

That is the message of this book.

You will read some astounding stories in these pages—all true. The stories reveal a world of risk and depravity and heartache that most of us have never touched.

Having personally experienced the fringes of Mary Frances's world, I believe these stories are themselves transformational. They smash through the walls of our comfortable, routine existence and flood us with the living, rapturous power of Jesus. It is the miraculous power that many read about in the Bible but rarely see in person. It is the power that comes when Jesus catches and holds the prostitute's gaze and says, "Neither do I condemn you…. Go now and leave your life of sin."

The need for this kind of transformation is so much greater than we realize. For example, over the past several years while conducting research for my books and other projects, I have been astounded to discover that there are women all around us who look as though they are living normal lives but are actually trapped in the sex industry. There are men all around us who are ensnared by its results. There are many people who look "together" on the outside but are dealing with deep wounds and struggles that need healing.

Is it really all that surprising that these stories exist? Anyone who has put on a "happy happy" face at church and pretended that their hurting marriage was fine can relate. Anyone who has been concerned that their coworker was doing drugs again, or that their teenage daughter might be sleeping with her boyfriend, can understand.

What you read in these pages will not only open your eyes and challenge you; it will give you hope. The same hope that the women in these stories have found. Sometimes that hope arrives instantly, and sometimes it requires years of taking two steps forward and one step back. But with Jesus, it always comes.

I'm thrilled that this book is now complete. Because once we vicariously live through the results of unconditional, nonjudgmental Christian love, once we watch Jesus change and transform those who have had no hope, not only are they dangerous for the kingdom…but we will be, too.

Shaunti Feldhahn

ACKNOWLEDGMENTS

I wish to extend a special thanks to the following people:

My family: Dick, Matt, Mandy, Paul, Mom, Dad, Mark, Candy, Joel, and Denise, for being a constant source of encouragement.

The five most dangerous women I know: Lynda, Helen, Jamie, Karen, and Amy, who have been on this dangerous journey from the beginning—through thick and thin!

Shaunti Feldhahn, for challenging me to write, walking me through the process, and connecting me with Bill Jensen and the great publishing team at Multnomah.

Jim Lund, who through many interviews and countless telephone calls and e-mails made these stories come alive and truly reflect the splendor of the Lord's work in each life.

Steffany Woolsey, for her editorial expertise and enthusiasm for this project.

Judy and the Wellspring Living Board of Directors for their support and encouragement.

Anna Marie, Gail, Ann, Sherry, Tammy, Nancy, and all of the intercessors who have been an integral part of the Wellspring journey.

Jenn, who faithfully worked with me as we began trying to put on paper the amazing works of God.

Victoria, for opening my eyes to the desperate plight of thousands of women and the need for a safe refuge for recovery.

The wonderful Wellspring Living staff.

The servant-hearted men and women of Fayette and Coweta counties who believed in the mission of Wellspring when we were just getting started.

And finally, all of the people who are included in this book. Thank you for allowing me to share God's work in you with the world!

INTRODUCTION

You know they're out there. You even see one occasionally. A woman dressed in leather and high heels, standing on a downtown street corner at night. A young lady slipping quietly into the back door of a strip club. A teenager with telltale needle marks on her arms.

They are desperate women living in a world of shadows. Most have known abuse, abandonment, and addiction their entire lives. Many feel trapped, with no hope of escape.

You would like to avoid them. They are dangerous.

Yet I have seen another side to many of these same women. They are courageously leaving behind their coping mechanisms—in fact, everything they've ever known—to trust in a faith they don't fully understand and a healing power they've yet to experience. Some are even taking this faith back to the streets, spreading the news about the forgiving, redeeming love of a Savior.

Also dangerous.

As director of Wellspring Living, a nonprofit ministry that helps broken women rebuild their lives, I work with these young ladies every day. I can't count the times I've been moved to tears by their circumstances and inspired by their perseverance. Each of them is a precious child in need of healing and hope. Each deserves compassion and love. And each was designed to bring glory to heaven—to be dangerous for God.

I consider these girls—along with Wellspring staff, volunteers, and board members—part of the league of dangerous women. They have found the courage to step out of reckless, desperate lifestyles and reach for the hand of Jesus. One by one, He is renewing these women, transforming them into warriors for His kingdom.

My prayer is that their stories will move you, too, to reach for Christ's hand—and to discover the powerful, healing, dangerous plans He has for you.

Mary Frances Bowley

A WORD ABOUT
WELLSPRING LIVING

Wellspring Living was founded in 2001 by a group of forty women with a desire to reach out to the greater Atlanta community. The core of this ministry is the Wellspring Home, which provides a safe place where motivated women who need a chance to start over can begin to rebuild their lives. Wellspring offers a no-cost residential program consisting of six months in an intensive therapeutic environment followed by six months of supported transition. Since its inception, more than seventy young women have benefited from this ministry.

Wellspring is also a network of volunteers and board members who serve through their prayers and through donations of time and funds. Some are mentors or teach classes to our program participants. Others work at one or both of our Wellspring Stores, upscale retail shops that sell donated merchandise to support the program's operating expenses. Still more help organize community events sponsored by Wellspring. In total, the ministry has more than fifteen hundred volunteers.

Most of the Wellspring program participants suffered from childhood sexual abuse or other traumas. By the time a young woman graduates from Wellspring, she has experienced healing for her past and the encouragement of a caring community, which equips her with life skills for her future. Yet the greatest gift she receives is an encounter with God and an understanding of the redemptive power and purpose of His love.

A LEAGUE OF
DANGEROUS
Women

1

KNOCKING ON THE DOOR

The first time I saw Danielle I had to close my eyes for a moment. She slouched next to a rusty Plymouth sedan wearing overalls and tennis shoes, both full of holes. Strands of greasy, dishwater-blond hair trickled out from underneath a tattered denim hat. Her shoulders sagged and her head was down. Everything about her seemed faded, lifeless, used up. She looked like a barren twig that would snap at the first hint of a strong breeze.

Only her eyes offered something more. She wouldn't look at me directly, but she stole an occasional glance at me from beneath her tattered hat. Once, her emerald eyes met mine, and I caught a glimpse of the emotions roiling inside.

She was scared.

So was I.

We were standing in the parking lot of a south side Atlanta condominium. Danielle had just driven up with every possession she owned—twelve black trash bags full of stale-smelling clothes and a puppy named Libby. At twenty-four, she was about to turn her life over to a pair of strangers.

I was one of those strangers. I had been director of women's ministries at First Baptist Church in Peachtree City, Georgia, for ten years. During the past few months, a group of us—me and forty women with a burning desire to please God—had discovered a common passion to reach out beyond the walls of our church to try to help women in need. We decided to call our new program *Wellspring,* after the living water Jesus promised to the Samaritan woman at the well. I was named director. Our idea was to connect with inner city missions and other ministries. We prayed about it many times; we were sure God was behind our enterprise.

As I shivered in the parking lot that cool December afternoon, however, I wondered just what I'd gotten myself into. Danielle had been physically, verbally, and sexually abused as a little girl. As an adult, her coping methods included forays into drinking, drugs, prostitution, and the occult. Five months earlier, she'd tried to take her own life. Friends put her in touch with a woman who had escaped the sex industry, and that contact led her to us.

Danielle hardly spoke a word, but the fact she'd shown up at all conveyed the plea behind her silence: *Everywhere I go, people take advantage of me. Are you the same as everybody else? Please, I need your help. I'm desperate. I just want someone to love me!*

The responsibility was almost overwhelming. I was confronting the flesh-and-blood reality of our outreach, and I didn't have a clue what to say.

"Danielle," I stammered, my heart beating double time, "it's so good to see you." Gently, I put my arm around her back to give her a hug, and caught a strong scent of musk and cigarette smoke. Danielle hugged me back—just a little. When I stepped away, I saw tears on her face. Whether they were from nervousness, excitement, relief, or a mix of all three, I couldn't tell.

Lord, I have nothing in common with this girl, I thought. *What am I going to say? I want to help, but what can I give her? Her needs are so great!*

I introduced Laura, our first Wellspring staff member who would live with Danielle for the next few months as her "coach." Slowly, measuring each step, Danielle followed us to the condominium we'd rented as her new home.

I understood her caution. She had been through so much pain. Danielle's uncle molested her when she was four. Her father, divorced from her mother, was in jail. Her mom lived from one drink and one destructive relationship to the next. On her seventeenth birthday, Danielle had run away from her North Carolina home with a boyfriend.

But life away from home merely deepened her nightmare. Danielle moved in with her boyfriend and his parents and siblings in Kansas. The boyfriend abused her physically and sexually. For a long time, she felt she couldn't leave because she feared the boyfriend or his brothers would hunt her down and kill her. Eventually, Danielle did escape and returned home to North Carolina—only to have her mother slam the front door in her face.

Danielle relied on drinking and drugs to distract her from the pain. She had no job and no education. A "friend" lured her into an escort service; prostitution soon became her means of financial support.

Finally, while the rest of the country celebrated Independence Day, Danielle decided she'd had enough. Miserable, hopeless, and feeling like a failure, she tried to end it all by swallowing a bottle of pills. That failed too.

A few months later, Danielle was arrested for driving with a suspended license. While in jail, with nothing else to do, she picked up a Bible for the first time and started reading it. Though she didn't understand most of the words, they had a strange impact on her. She felt a sensation she'd almost forgotten existed—a faint flicker of hope.

After Danielle was released, she asked a Christian guy she'd met if he'd take her to church with him. That evening, she cried through the entire service, even the skit about Jesus knocking on the door of unbelievers' hearts. She wanted whatever it was these people had, something that was missing in her own life. She dared to hope.

Two days later, alone in her sister's home, Danielle literally opened the front door to the house and said, "Okay, Jesus, You can come in now. Will You be my best friend? Will You walk with me forever?"

Now, as I watched Danielle tearfully unwrap the welcome basket Laura and I had prepared for her at the condominium, I wondered how I would ever connect with this brave, scarred, vulnerable, searching young woman. *How can I relate to her, Lord? How will she ever learn to trust me?*

Our backgrounds were so different. I'd grown up in a strong Christian home and attended every church activity on the calendar—choir practices, mission programs, vacation Bible schools; Danielle didn't believe in God as a child and never set foot in a house of worship. My idyllic grade school years featured football games, fort building, and roller skating parties in the driveway with friends; Danielle spent much of her early years stuck in her bedroom listening to her mom's drinking parties. I married my high school sweetheart in my hometown church in front of five bridesmaids and grooms-men and a packed church; Danielle snuck out of a bedroom window in the middle of the night to run off with a boyfriend who beat and raped her.

Danielle was the kind of girl that, when I was a child, I'd been taught to stay as far from as possible. She wasn't a "nice girl." She would only lead to trouble.

She was dirty.

Different.

Dangerous.

We led Danielle on a quick tour of the condo—two bed-rooms, the bathroom, the pantry. The farther we walked, the more she seemed to shrink into herself, as if she wanted to melt right into the carpet.

Still, I thought, *maybe we're not so different.*

Danielle had learned early in life how cruel the world can be. But I'd seen some of that cruelty too, like the times kids had mercilessly teased my oldest brother, Robert, calling him "retard" because he had Down's syndrome. Once, while skipping rope on the school playground when I was in first grade, I heard one of Robert's third-grade classmates yell that he was "dumb." Then he pushed Robert—twice. I was too mad to be afraid. I marched over and gave that much-taller bully a bloody nose.

Then there was the fact that time and again, people close to Danielle—the people she should have been able to depend on most—had betrayed her. Her father walked out of her life. Her mother ignored her. Her uncle molested her. Her boyfriend abused her.

I also knew something about betrayal. After nine years of what I thought was a strong marriage, I discovered that my husband was having an affair. My whole world fell apart. He took her and his paid-for, fire-engine-red Ford truck and left me with house payments, car payments, two dogs, and a five-month-old baby. Only the Lord's comforting presence got me through those dark days.

And then there was God Himself. For most of her life, Danielle had experienced an emptiness and hopelessness that seemed to stretch to the stars. But sitting in a lonely jail cell, she read for the first time about a Messiah and found a shred of hope. Now she was on a quest to find out everything she could about this amazing, loving, personal Savior named Jesus.

Yes, I had grown up in the church, read Scripture, practiced my devotions, and led women's Bible studies for years. But I too had come to a place of frustration and emptiness. It seemed as if I and the other women in our church loved each other well, and even loved God well. But how close could we be to God's heart if we didn't touch the people Jesus wanted us to touch, the "least of these"? I sensed there was more to my relationship with God than what I was experiencing. I also had engaged in a quest to discover everything the Lord had in store for me—and I believed it started with reaching out to the helpless and downtrodden.

We finished our tour of the condo and sat down at the dining room table to establish rules for our new arrangement. Danielle agreed to all our conditions and signed a "contract." She gave me another furtive glance, but this time I thought I detected the barest hint of a smile.

Just maybe, I thought, *we have more in common than I realized.*

That first week was a hard one for Danielle. She wanted everything to fall into place. She especially wanted her family to be normal and to just love her. She asked if she could go home for Christmas; we said no. Her mother, Jackie, had already called the woman at the emergency shelter, cussed her out, and told her we were wasting our time on her daughter. I felt a home visit would be toxic for Danielle—too much, too soon.

We did agree that her mother could meet her at a restaurant a few days before Christmas. On a Saturday, I picked Danielle up at the condo and drove to a Chili's for our appointment. We sat down in the receiving area to wait. I could see that she was excited and nervous. We'd already replaced much of her wardrobe and given her a makeover and haircut. Now she wore a stunning new black-and-red pantsuit. Already the lifeless figure I'd observed just days before was transforming into the beautiful girl within.

While we made small talk and watched the clock, Danielle repeatedly rubbed her hands together. She couldn't sit still. As ten minutes passed—then twenty—then thirty—I had a hard time keeping still myself.

Finally, Danielle recognized a young woman walking toward us. It was her twin sister, Deanna.

"Hi, Danielle," she said, looking me over out of the corner of her eye. "Uh, Mom got into a fight with Larry. She said she's too upset and she can't come."

I turned to Danielle in time to see her face crumple. All the pent-up emotion that had been building since our arrival seemed to escape like air from a balloon. She stared at the floor.

I felt my heart breaking right along with hers.

A few minutes later I sat in a nearby booth, watching the two sisters talk, and tried to get a handle on my emotions. *Lord,* I prayed, *I told Jackie this would be her only chance to see Danielle before Christmas. Surely she understands how much Danielle wants her to be a part of her life. Christmas is such a special time for parents and their children. How could a mother not show up to see her daughter?*

I knew I couldn't be the mother Danielle needed, but I prayed that God would show me how to help however I could.

One idea came to me a few days later. I'd had Danielle over at my home for a reunion with her Great Dane–Labrador mix, Libby. She loved that dog. Libby was probably the only creature on earth that had shown Danielle unconditional love. We'd found a couple willing to take care of Libby while Danielle stayed at Wellspring, so it was a wonderful surprise for Danielle to see her again. Libby slurped Danielle's face so many times I thought I'd need a hose to wipe off the saliva. I snapped a picture of the two of them sitting happily in front of our Christmas tree.

On Christmas Eve, I brought Danielle over again. I knew how hard it was for her to be without family, and as much as possible, I wanted to give her a sense of belonging. She joined me and my husband, Dick, my sons, Paul and Matt, and Matt's girlfriend on a drive through the neighborhood to look at Christmas lights. The beautiful reds, greens, blues, and whites on every house twinkled just as a certain star over Bethlehem may have on that night so many years ago. Danielle's face glowed too as she took it all in.

Then we gathered around the kitchen table and handed out Christmas presents. We had no gold, incense, or myrrh, yet the love behind each package was just as sincere as the gifts of the Magi. When Danielle's turn came, I watched her unwrap the photo I'd had enlarged and framed of her and Libby by the Christmas tree.

It was such a small thing, but when I saw the tears flow down her cheeks I knew it had also been the right thing. I got up and gave her a hug, my own eyes misting over.

"Thank you," she whispered, looking back and forth between the picture and me. "This is one of my best Christmas gifts ever."

It was, I felt, one of God's tiny miracles. Danielle was

gradually opening up her heart, trusting us more and allowing us to love her.

We encountered another miracle a couple of weeks later. We'd received more calls about young women seeking to escape the sex industry and other unhealthy situations. These girls desperately needed a place to stay. We were already assisting Danielle. Now we felt the Lord leading us to establish a home for young women who needed godly support. We could be the bridge for these girls on their journey to Jesus.

Just after Christmas, I contacted a builder friend. Did he know of a place that might suit our need? It turned out that a couple was moving out of a secluded, 4,600-square-foot model home—one he'd "always thought should be used for ministry." Before I knew it, someone was volunteering to make a first payment, and the owner was handing me the keys. We were landlords; our tenants would be the "poor and the needy and the brokenhearted" (Psalm 109:16). It was a staggering responsibility—but if God was behind it, who was I to argue?

Danielle and Laura moved into the new home in January. We invited Danielle to decorate her room however she wanted, keeping in mind that girls like herself would one day be living there. A week or so later, I was astounded to see what she'd done. The room was painted a bright purple, so that anyone staying there would "know they are royalty." Even more significant, the walls were adorned with Bible verses, all neatly transcribed in silver.

Behind the door, I saw the verse that I knew had changed

Danielle's life: "Behold, I stand at the door and knock. If any-one hears My voice and opens the door, I will come in to him and dine with him, and he with Me" (Revelation 3:20, NKJV).

"Danielle," I said, turning slowly to take in the full effect, "this looks fantastic."

"These are the verses that have meant so much to me," Danielle said. "I want to be able to lay here and see Him and hear Him. I want everyone who comes here after me to know that Jesus is here, that He's speaking to them too."

I was so proud of her—and so grateful that Jesus was moving in her heart.

Over the next several weeks, I watched the Lord continue to work on the heart of this earnest new member of His family. Danielle struggled at times with Bible studies. She faced other struggles too. We were all baffled when she sud-denly began responding to Laura's every word and deed with hostility. This went on for weeks, until we discovered that the trigger had been a moment when Laura turned her body a certain way. Danielle didn't realize it at the time, but it reminded her of her mother and the abuse she'd suffered.

Yet through the difficulties, Danielle was clearly making progress. The reason, I had no doubt, was her determination to rely on the Lord. There was the time I showed up intend-ing to take Danielle shopping. Laura informed me, however, that Danielle probably wouldn't be speaking to me. She'd decided to break her cigarette addiction by spending the day reading the Bible.

I changed my agenda, and we soon found a quiet place for Danielle to allow God's Word to wash over her. I checked on her periodically throughout the day. I'd never seen anyone become so filled with peace and joy from reading Scripture. Danielle wasn't just putting to death a destructive habit; she was coming back to life.

Danielle was, in fact, changing in many wonderful ways. She smiled more often. She grew more relaxed and confident. She was transforming into a strikingly beautiful girl. Best of all, she was maturing spiritually, drawing closer every day to the Lord.

The astonishing thing was that as I watched and participated in Danielle's change, I found myself changing too. I saw how fragile life was. I started treating people with more care, more love. As my husband and I prayed together for Danielle, I felt our marriage growing stronger, our relationship going deeper.

Walking through the pain with a broken girl who had no hope, who had just wanted to die, and seeing God lead her into a life filled with joy and meaning was incredible. My faith soared into the clouds. I now saw—I *felt* in the depths of my soul—that God could do anything. I was privileged to watch the love of Jesus in action. I was seeing, as my husband likes to say, "God with skin on."

The full impact of what God was doing in all our lives hit me during a Good Friday service in the same church where Danielle had cried through a skit about Jesus. Anyone who had seen her then wouldn't have recognized her on this day. Her steps were quick and lively. Her face radiated peace.

Deanna, Danielle's twin sister, and Deanna's husband and four-year-old son accompanied us that evening. They'd never been in a church before. The service and worship gathered momentum. Soon we were singing "Amazing Love" at the top of our lungs while watching a video presentation of the crucifixion.

Out of the corner of my eye—in the same way Danielle had once warily peered at me—I stole a glance at her standing next to me. She was singing and smiling, her arms stretched toward the rafters. A steady stream of tears flowed down her face.

What really got me, though, was seeing Deanna and her son next to Danielle. Both were watching Danielle intently. The look on Deanna's face, a combination of surprise and envy, seemed to say, *I want what she has!*

The little boy had his hands in the air. He was trying to worship just like Danielle.

Tears blurred my vision as I lifted my own arms higher to Him. It occurred to me that Danielle was still dangerous. But she wasn't dangerous to me. She was a warrior for the kingdom, turning souls toward heaven simply by seeking holiness.

Now she was dangerous for God.

Lord, I prayed, *thank You so much—this is the greatest blessing of my life! Thank You for giving me a heart for the brokenhearted, for giving me a desire to free the prisoners and help You turn mourning into joy. Thank You for the forty sisters in Christ who share this vision and who are such an encouragement to me. Thank You for Laura, who has given so much of her time and love to Danielle these last few months. And thank You for Danielle, for leading us to each other, and for allowing me to love her.*

Thank You, God, that You have brought us all together—a league of dangerous women—to give all the glory to You. Amen!

∼

In 2002, Danielle moved in with a loving host family as the first "graduate" of the Wellspring program. She married in 2004 and is completing an internship at a hair salon. She and her husband live in Atlanta with their Great Dane, Annabelle.

Danielle says she still struggles at times with issues from her past, but God is leading her through it all. "Sometimes," she says, "I ask myself, after all the terrible things I've done, 'How could God love me?' But He's teaching me what unconditional love is. He won't leave, and He won't let me pull away. I love God with all my heart. He's the only thing I've found in my entire life that's true and safe. He's always knocking on my door."

2

Skylar

IT WAS LOVE

The leaves on the maple and ash trees lining the street had transformed into vibrant reds and purples on the fall afternoon Skylar bounced off the school bus. She'd just finished her first day of first grade. Her long, blond hair flowing behind her, Skylar ran to the front door of her Baltimore home and let herself in.

The house was quiet. Skylar hurried to her mother's bedroom door and opened it. As usual, the lights were off and the shades drawn. Her mother lay with her back to the doorway.

"Mommy, I'm back from school!" Skylar called. She wanted to tell her mother everything.

Her mother stirred but said nothing.

Skylar's thoughts rushed back to that morning, when she'd first walked into her new classroom. It seemed as if all the other first graders were surrounded by smiling parents who took pictures and helped their children to their seats.

Skylar had to walk alone around the room until she found her name scrawled on one of the desks. How she'd wished her mother had come with her.

Skylar blinked away the memory and the tears that had started to form. She moved to the other side of the bed. Donna Olshansky's eyes were shut.

"Mommy, would you come outside and play with me?" Skylar asked. "Please? The sun's out. It's warm."

Donna moved her lips, but no sound came out. Her eyes remained closed. Finally, softly, the words arrived: "Not today, Skylar. I'm too tired."

Skylar crawled under the blankets with her mother—as she had so often before, as she would so many times in the years ahead—and gently placed her head on her mother's stomach. She could hear it growling underneath her mother's nightgown.

Skylar sighed. *Please, Mommy,* she thought, *couldn't you get up and play this time? Please?*

For Skylar, it was just another lonely afternoon. Her mother suffered from a multiple personality disorder, battled severe depression, and spent much of her time in bed. Her father, a gambler and alcoholic with a temper, had not lived with the rest of the family since before Skylar was born. When he did show up, usually without notifying them, he was physically and verbally abusive. Debbie, Skylar's oldest sister, was often out of the house, busy with her own friends. Her younger sister, Nancy, was just a toddler.

Vicki, who was two years older than Skylar, tried to be a mother for her younger sister, but she was hardly qualified to raise another child. Far too often Skylar had to fend for herself. When she played "house" with her friends, she never asked to be the mommy—she wanted to be the daughter. It was just play, but for a few minutes, at least, she could pretend that someone was taking care of her. She only wanted someone to notice her—to love her.

God was missing from Skylar's life too. Donna loved to read from the Bible when she was able, but she rarely had the energy to take Skylar to church. For Skylar, there was no personal connection with God. She believed in Him in a distant way, but didn't see Him as part of her daily life. He didn't seem to care about her personally. But then, no one did.

With so little adult supervision, it wasn't surprising that Skylar and her sisters experimented with alcohol and drugs. Skylar started drinking at age ten. She tried marijuana the following year.

When she was thirteen and faced with the prospect of another boring weekend, Skylar went to the beach with a friend of her sister's and the friend's boyfriend. She took a walk along the water with the boyfriend. As they talked, he pulled a bag of white powder out of his pocket and rolled it up inside a dollar bill.

It was heroin.

After a long sniff, the boyfriend held out the bill toward Skylar.

"Want to try it? It's good stuff."

Skylar hesitated for only a moment. She'd never done any hard drugs, but she liked hanging out with her sister's friends, and she was curious about what heroin would be like. She nodded.

Skylar tried a few sniffs. Soon a warm, happy feeling surged through her. Skylar felt like a balloon floating up to the clouds. Her skin flushed and her mouth grew dry, but she didn't care—the peaceful sensation was wonderful. She wanted more.

Over the next two years, she found more. Skylar began making new friends. She went to parties. She met a guy who sold drugs and immediately hit it off with him. Stuart was cute—tall, tan, with blond hair—five years older, and an artist. Best of all, he seemed to like and care about Skylar. It wasn't long before they were a couple and having sex.

Is this love? Skylar asked herself one morning in bed. She liked Stuart, but it seemed as if there should be something more. She wondered if she was even capable of love.

Vicki had been angry when she found out her sister was taking heroin. But Skylar didn't care. She was infatuated with the euphoric feeling the drug gave her. She'd found an escape from her lonely, hopeless life—a new world to call home.

Skylar was fifteen when she noticed her clothes fitting more tightly. She'd also felt a little queasy the last few days. Surely she couldn't be—no, that wasn't possible. She didn't even want to think about it.

But she would check it out. Just to make sure.

After a trip to the grocery store, Skylar sat cross-legged on her bathroom counter, waiting for the results—waiting on the little white stick that had the power to change her life. She felt her heart rate rise and her cheeks flush. She stared at the wall clock, willing the minute hand to move faster.

Finally, the ten minutes were up. Skylar slowly lowered

her gaze to the stick folded within her trembling hand.

Positive.

Positive? How can it be positive? There's nothing positive *about it!*

She looked in the mirror. Staring back at her was the face of a scared teenager. She quickly brushed a tear away. She'd learned a long time ago that crying didn't change anything. This was her problem and she would deal with it.

Skylar told Stuart. He wasn't happy about it; he said he would pay for an abortion. Skylar didn't know what else to do, so she agreed to the plan. She told a friend of her sister's who helped schedule an appointment at a clinic.

Skylar told no one else about the pregnancy. Her mother and sisters would be shocked and ashamed. Her father would be furious—who knew what he'd do if he found out? She felt so alone, but there was nothing she could do about it.

As the appointment at the clinic approached, Skylar cried often. She began to wonder if she was doing the right thing. *I can't have a baby, I can't raise a child,* she reasoned. *But do I really want an abortion?*

At the clinic, a sonogram showed that Skylar was eight weeks along. She made an appointment to have the abortion in two weeks.

A couple of days later, Skylar was alone in her bedroom. She was high on heroin, and crying again. She was miserable. There was a terrible, almost physical pressure inside her.

I've messed up everything in my life already, she thought. *I can't let them know I'm pregnant too. I have to get this abortion. What else can I do?*

A memory suddenly filled Skylar's mind. When Skylar was very young, her oldest sister, Debbie, had been pregnant. Skylar hadn't entirely understood what was going on, but she knew that Debbie had delivered the baby and given it up for adoption.

Adoption? Could I really do that?

Skylar stopped crying and thought about it. The more she thought, the more the pressure inside of her relented. By the end of the afternoon, she'd made a decision: She would have the baby and give it to parents who could offer her child a better life, a life with hope.

For the first time in weeks, she felt a hint of peace.

Thanks to fervent prayers by many people, Skylar's mother was recovering from her years-long struggles with her depression and personality disorder. Donna decided to move to the Atlanta area for a fresh start; Skylar chose to go with her. Only after they'd moved did she tell her mother about the child she was carrying, and her wish to give it up for adoption. Her mother was surprisingly supportive. She agreed that adoption was the best choice.

Like her mother, Skylar also wanted a fresh start. She was clearly showing when she tried to enroll in a public high school in an Atlanta suburb, but school officials there discouraged her.

"I think it would be better for everyone, honey, if you enrolled in a night school," one administrator said. Skylar got the message. As an unwed mother-to-be, she was a disgrace, something to be kept out of sight.

The weeks leading up to the birth were like a dream to

Skylar. She felt disconnected from the tiny being growing inside of her. It was too much to take in, the idea that she was bringing a life into the world. But she liked the way her baby felt when it turned or kicked its legs. It reminded her that she wasn't alone in the world anymore.

On a muggy afternoon in late April, Skylar went to a doctor's office for a checkup. The baby was due in two weeks. "Oh my gosh," the nurse said. "You're seven and a half centimeters dilated. We need to get you to the hospital."

Skylar's baby seemed determined to set a speed record. After just a few contractions, the hospital staff broke Skylar's water and gave her an epidural. Half an hour later, she was holding her beautiful baby girl.

To Skylar, the sight and touch of her baby was like waking up for the first time in her life. She had beautiful brown eyes and wisps of dark hair on her head. Skylar felt immediate and inexpressible devotion. She savored every look, every moment of contact: perfect, miniature arms and legs that wiggled and kicked in a wonderful, chaotic dance; shallow, warm baby breaths that tickled her neck; a tiny, wondering face with eyes that darted to every movement.

All her life, Skylar had guarded her heart and her feelings. To survive, she'd had to. But now a dam was bursting inside her. She couldn't hold back the flood if she wanted to. The feeling overwhelmed her, filling every nook and cranny of her being.

It was love. It was wonderful. And it was all directed at this fragile form in her arms.

When Skylar held out a single finger, her daughter's arm

swung up and—for just a fleeting instant—wrapped chubby little fingers around it. Then she let go. Skylar laughed, but the laugh caught in her throat. She remembered that all too soon, she would be forced to do the same.

For two days at the hospital, Skylar showered undivided attention on her adorable baby daughter. For the first time, she wondered what her child's life would be like, what dreams she would dream, what worlds she would conquer. As she thought about it, a distant cloud of despair grew blacker and thicker. Skylar would not be a daily presence in her daughter's life. The adoption they'd arranged was an open one. Skylar would be able to contact her daughter. But she would miss so much—nearly everything.

Adoption was the right thing to do, the most loving thing. But the thought of it was breaking the heart Skylar had only just discovered she had.

Suddenly, it was time. The couple that Skylar and her mother had picked out were in the room. Byron was a tall, fifty-ish pastor. Lisa was a proper Southern wife with dark hair and a sweet smile. At the moment, Skylar didn't like them at all.

After a few awkward moments of conversation, a nurse stepped beside the bed where Skylar held her baby. She was wrapped in a soft paisley blanket decorated with tiny blue elephants.

Skylar made no move to give her up. Tears ran down her cheeks. She cleared her throat and looked at Lisa. "What…what is her name?"

"Elizabeth," Lisa said quietly, still standing a few feet away. "Elizabeth Marie."

Skylar could no longer contain herself. The sobs came loud and hard. Teardrops splashed onto Elizabeth's face and the blue elephants.

"Please, Skylar," the nurse said gently. "It's time."

Skylar wailed and shook her head. But when the nurse slowly and tenderly put out her arms to gather up the baby, Skylar did not resist. She loved her daughter so much—yet she knew she had to let her go.

It was so strange to see her daughter—*Elizabeth*—in the arms of this stranger. Lisa smiled at the bundle in the blanket, and then she looked back to Skylar. Her face wore an odd mixture of joy, hope, and sadness. Lisa stared intently at Skylar for a moment, then turned her back and walked out of the room.

Just like that, they were gone.

Her baby was gone.

~

Everything changed for Skylar after the birth of her daughter. Finding real love for the first time—and then losing it—was more than she could bear. Despite the hardships she faced as a child, Skylar had been outgoing and talkative. Now it was as if she'd collapsed into herself. She had nothing to live for.

Skylar returned to Baltimore, where she moved in with a new group of friends and finished high school. But her memories of Elizabeth—too sacred for common recollection, too painful to reflect on for long—haunted her. Finally, she turned to an old "friend" for comfort: heroin.

Depression and drugs fed off one another. The worse

Skylar felt, the more she needed a heroin high; the more drugs she took, the deeper she slipped into the abyss of hopelessness. Soon, everything revolved around heroin. She couldn't wake up without getting high. She couldn't go to work or to sleep without it. If she went more than a few hours without a fix, she became violently sick.

She was an addict.

For two years, Skylar fed her addiction. She worked two jobs and borrowed money from friends to pay for the drugs. She stopped paying her bills. Her skin turned a grayish green. Her apartment was a disaster—flies buzzing around stacks of dirty dishes, maggots crawling inside the stove, cats defecating in every room—but Skylar hardly noticed.

$\sim$

It was a Saturday, a day like any other, when Skylar awoke and crawled into the bathroom to begin her morning routine. The high from the night before was already fading. She needed more.

Skylar filled a syringe, wrapped the tie from her bathrobe around her upper left arm, and slapped a vein a couple times with the palm of her right hand. Her veins had always been difficult to find, but this morning it was impossible. She worked for several minutes, her attempts at inserting the needle growing more frantic. She drew blood from both arms, but couldn't pierce the scar tissue.

She slumped onto the floor. *I'm so pathetic I can't even get high.*

She started to sob, then pounded her fist on a cabinet.

Her whole life she'd taken care of herself because there was no one else to do the job. But now, bleeding on her bathroom floor, she had nothing left.

"God, I can't do this anymore! You have to help me!"

Skylar didn't hear an answer—but that desperate prayer gave voice to a new purpose. She would stop. No matter what it took, no matter how much help she needed from others, she would stop.

She was going to get clean.

Soon after, Skylar moved in with an aunt back in Georgia. The aunt had lost a son to heroin. For the next seven days and nights, Skylar endured chills, sweats, vomiting, and panic attacks. She felt completely out of control; jitters and irritability nearly drove her mad. Her skin crawled and her muscles cramped. Her body convulsed no matter how tightly she curled up. It was a week of pure torture. Then, for the following ten days, Skylar couldn't sleep. Her body, exhausted and limp from fatigue, would not rest until the chemical imbalances inside returned to normal.

The only relief came when she called her mother. Donna read Scripture and prayed with Skylar over the phone. For those few moments, Skylar felt a sense of peace and love that she realized was coming from God. In some ways, it was the same kind of "high" that she got from heroin. Yet Skylar knew it was also completely different. God wouldn't turn on her and leave her in pain and despair the way heroin did.

This was real love—the kind Skylar had tasted when Elizabeth was born, the kind she'd been searching for all her life. And she wanted more.

When Donna heard about Wellspring and told Skylar about our program, they decided it was exactly what she needed to help her get back on her feet and learn more about God. She was accepted, and in April 2003, just after Skylar turned twenty, she joined us.

I met Skylar for the first time on her second day in the home. She'd just finished lunch and was coming out of the dining room as I entered the front hallway. I was struck by how beautiful she was—and how wounded she appeared. She was incredibly thin. Her long, blond hair almost covered her face, and her shoulders curled inward. When I spoke to her, she didn't smile or look me in the eye. She reminded me of a hurt puppy.

"You must be Skylar," I said. "I'm Mary Frances Bowley. I'm so glad you're here."

"Thank you for having me," she said quietly.

Lord, I prayed after we parted, *I've never seen anyone quite so beautiful and so polite. But I know underneath that "all together" exterior is a hurting young woman. Please give us special discernment to help Skylar heal her hidden wounds.*

In the following months, Skylar was in many ways a model member of the group. She eagerly soaked in every word during Bible classes. During discussion sessions, she frequently offered wise advice to the girls in the home. She seemed to have an instinct for identifying the problems other girls were having and what needed to be done about them.

When it came to her own needs, however, Skylar was less forthcoming. She often hid her pain behind walls of reserve and competency. Even after several months in the program, she would sometimes go without food rather than tell anyone she was hungry.

Gradually, however, cracks began to appear in Skylar's walls. When playing board games with the other girls, she could be silly and playful. She slowly began to open up. Despite her self-sufficient nature, honed by years of necessity, she was determined to learn how to trust others and give God control of her life.

The Lord blessed Skylar for her sincere heart. She landed a position as an intern with a church program for children in Atlanta's inner city. It was a perfect match. She loved working with the younger kids, and quickly formed a bond with the most rebellious ones. When she stopped in their neighborhood, they dropped whatever they were doing and ran to her for hugs.

Skylar's favorite was a five-year-old named Corey. Whenever he was around her, he jumped up and down, shouting, "Hold me! Hold me! Hold me!" Once, when Skylar came to pick him up for an event at the church, he was sick and vomiting—but still begging to come with her. He slept with his head in her lap through the entire program.

Skylar graduated from the Wellspring program in 2004, but it was at a reunion event a few months later that I realized just how much progress she'd made, and how much God was continuing to work in her life.

The reunion involving ten graduates and a handful of staff and volunteers had lasted through the summer weekend. Now it was Sunday afternoon, and time for the final event of our celebration. Sunbeams slanted through the living room windows at the Wellspring Home, adding warmth to the gathering. One at a time, each graduate was asked to sit in a chair in the middle of the room. Then three or four of our volunteer "prayer warriors" gathered around and petitioned the Lord on behalf of that graduate. It was a moving experience for each of them.

Skylar sat in a corner of the room, observing intently as always. Finally, it was her turn. She was the last graduate to be honored.

For Skylar, however, the rules were changed. Mary, one of our volunteers, removed the chair and asked Skylar to stand in the center of the room. Then Mary explained what was going to happen next.

"I want you all to come up here and form a circle around Skylar," she said. "The Israelites brought down the walls of Jericho by walking around it seven times and shouting. We're going to do the same thing and bring down Skylar's walls."

Mary explained that everyone was to walk in a circle around Skylar seven times, praying as they walked. After the seventh time, all would shout, jump, praise God, and celebrate with Skylar—and Skylar was expected to join in as well.

While Mary talked, Skylar stood in the middle of the circle, hands clasped, with an "I don't know if I'm up for this" look on her face. But as the group stepped and prayed around her, Skylar's expression slowly changed. She dropped her hands to her sides. It was as if she were finally shedding the skin that had protected her for so long—and that had blocked the love and compassion others wanted to shower on her.

By the start of the group's seventh pass around her, Skylar was actually smiling in anticipation. When it was done, a yell that must have been heard across Atlanta echoed through the house. Everyone laughed, giggled, and thanked God for what He was doing in Skylar's life.

Skylar laughed and shouted with them.

~

Today, at age twenty-three, Skylar is a valuable member of the Wellspring staff. Her intuition about others serves her well in intake interviews and when she conducts our Twelve Steps Recovery, Art Therapy, and Beginning Christianity classes. Her experience as a recovering addict allows her to encourage girls from the same background.

Skylar is still working to reconcile that background with her new life. As much as she wants to see Elizabeth, it's been four years since they last met. The agony of saying good-bye remains more than she can bear. Skylar is also still learning about love, but the Lord is teaching her. She knows that He loves her, that He'll never abandon her, and that even when He disciplines her it is because of His great love for her. When she thinks about God giving up His Son on the cross, she remembers the pain of giving up Elizabeth—and she feels at least a hint of understanding of the depth of His love.

"God is just amazing," she says. "He's changed everything for me. I know I'll never go away from Him."

What is most amazing to me now is watching Skylar pour out her love on others. She still adores children and wants to work with kids who are addicted to drugs. She also looks forward to marrying and becoming a mother again. She wants six kids and plans to adopt some of them.

The girl who once felt so unnoticed and unloved, who didn't know if she even *could* love others, now has an unlimited supply. I never get tired of seeing God's miracles. This one was born out of love.

3

HE WILL TAKE CARE OF YOU

One hot afternoon last summer, I sat down with Meredith in a Waffle House restaurant north of Atlanta. As always, Meredith's appearance was striking. She wore a fashionable black dress that perfectly matched her braided hair and dark skin. Six feet tall and graceful, she could easily pass for a model.

The only piece of the puzzle that didn't fit this glamorous exterior was the item next to her in our booth. It was a tiny car seat, and tucked inside the seat was Meredith's four-month-old baby, Christian.

"He's adorable," I said as Christian yawned and closed his eyes.

"Thank you. I think so too—especially when he's sleeping like this," Meredith said with a laugh. She gently pulled a blanket up close to her son's face and tenderly rocked his car seat.

She's going to be a wonderful mother—again, I thought. Meredith had always been a nurturer, adept at taking care of others. If only the people around her had been as good at taking care of her…

～

Meredith was raised in a home in New York with twelve brothers and sisters. She knew that her parents loved her, but in their large family, with people constantly coming and going, she often felt overlooked.

That was never more true than on the day her uncle sexually molested her. She was six years old. Ervin told Meredith that he would "hurt her bad" if she ever told anyone what he'd done. He beat her to prove his point, so she kept quiet.

The abuse and the beatings continued. Finally, after three years, the family moved away from New York and Meredith's uncle to Richmond, Virginia. Meredith felt she was safe at last, but her relief was short-lived. An older brother began to sexually abuse her. He threatened to kill her if anyone found out.

Most children who are victims of sexual abuse have trouble setting boundaries later in life. They grow up feeling powerless. It's as if they lose the ability to say no.

Meredith was no different. She became sexually active with other boys and was pregnant at age fifteen. Nine months later, she had a son she named Taylor.

Meredith's family members were Jehovah's Witnesses, but Meredith was dissociated from the church when elders there discovered she was pregnant. She felt abandoned.

She didn't get much support from her family either. There were just too many kids and too many problems. Though she was only sixteen, she decided to move out with her son and live with a sister of Taylor's father.

"You'll be back," Meredith's mother told her. "It's tough out there."

It *was* tough, but Meredith never did move home. Instead, at nineteen, she married Atiku, a Nigerian ten years her senior. Meredith believes now she was looking as much for a protector as she was a husband—someone who would take care of her and her son.

Both Meredith and her husband struggled with the marriage. Meredith knew little of Nigerian customs. They had trouble communicating. Meredith was unhappy, yet she put on a mask and tried to act is if everything were all right. She was angry and bitter about the sexual abuse in her past, and often had nightmares about it. Yet she never told Atiku. She was sure something terrible would happen if she revealed her secret.

After six years, Meredith and Atiku divorced. The hard times continued for Meredith. Looking for a fresh start, she hooked up with a boyfriend and moved with him to Atlanta, but the relationship didn't last. She tried to start a small business, but it never got off the ground. She wrote out plans to launch a ministry for the poor, then grew discouraged and gave up. Lacking career training, she took whatever jobs were available to support herself and Taylor.

When she was thirty and Taylor was fourteen, Meredith was laid off her job as a secretary. She'd always been able to find something when she'd lost jobs before, but this time every effort failed. When a friend offered her money to substitute as an "escort" for businessmen, she naively said yes. It was the beginning of a descent into the ugly world of prostitution.

Once it began, Meredith felt trapped. She couldn't see a way to quit and continue to provide for herself and Taylor. Yet the pain, guilt, and shame were overwhelming. She tried to hide what she was doing from her son, and felt like a hypocrite because of it.

Why did I do this? she asked herself over and over. *How did I get to this point?*

When a friend, also an escort, became so depressed that she killed herself with a gun, Meredith realized she was in deep trouble. She had to do something—but what?

The only bright spot in her troubled life was a man named Julius. He was a comedian with a dazzling smile that she'd met at Echelon, an Atlanta nightclub where he was performing. They'd dated for a time, but Julius had broken it off when he discovered Meredith was in the escort business. Since then, however, he'd remained a loyal friend.

One day, while they were having lunch in a restaurant, Julius asked the question Meredith had feared all her life.

"Meredith, I've seen certain signs with you," he said quietly. "I don't know how else to ask you this, and I want you to know I'm asking as a friend. Have you ever been sexually abused?"

Immediately, Meredith's back stiffened. She fought off the impulse to run. *How does he know? What will he do?* Yet when she looked in Julius's eyes, there was no condemnation. She saw only compassion.

She covered her face with her hands. She was thirty, but felt like a terrified child. In a small voice, she answered, "Yes."

For the first time, Meredith explained what had happened to her so many years before. Julius just listened, his eyes glistening. Meredith still felt scared now that her secret was out. But she also felt a huge wave of relief. Finally, she could share her burden with someone else.

With encouragement from Julius, Meredith stopped escorting and began seeing a counselor. But as the feelings she'd suppressed for so long came out, she went into a deep depression. She spent most of her days in bed. Taylor had to prepare their meals when he came home from school.

Emotionally and financially, it was too much for Meredith. She stopped meeting with her counselor. She returned to the escort business.

Julius was afraid for Meredith, but didn't feel he was helping any longer. "I think we need to be away from each other for a while," he said. "I will always be your friend, but I believe this is what God wants me to do."

Meredith was losing control. She didn't have enough money. She couldn't seem to function. Then, on a Thursday, Meredith came home from work to find a notice on the door of her apartment. It said her complex was under new management, and that her lease would not be renewed.

Meredith knew she was late with her rent payment, but the previous owners had always allowed her to stay if she added a late fee to her check. She hurried to the apartment complex office.

"I'll have the money soon," she explained. "I can pay a late fee."

"Ma'am, I'm sorry," the woman there said. "We're new management, and we're not renewing your lease. Just so you know, anything that's still in the apartment on Tuesday will be moved out into the street."

Meredith was devastated. If she lost the apartment, she knew she'd have to send Taylor to live with his father in Philadelphia. She'd already lost Julius. Now she was losing her home and her son. What was left?

Painful as it was, Meredith did send Taylor away. There was no other choice. She moved in with Janelle, a friend who was also an escort. The months passed by like a blur. Meredith felt she was operating on autopilot. She'd lost hope.

One night, while talking with Janelle at the apartment, Meredith felt she'd reached the end of herself. Finally she was ready to say no to the prison that was her life.

"Janelle, I don't know what I'm going to do, but this is it for me," she said. "I'm done with escorting."

Meredith's friend studied her face and saw the determination there. "I believe you," she said.

Out of the blue—or perhaps out of a prompting from heaven—Meredith thought of Julius. She hadn't spoken to him for almost a year. On impulse, she left him a phone message and said she'd like to talk. Two days later, they were sitting across from one another in a restaurant.

Meredith was so glad to see him. Julius had always been there for her. Yet she couldn't tell him about losing Taylor and her apartment. She was too ashamed.

Eventually, however, Julius figured out that something was wrong. "Meredith, I will always be your friend," he said. "You can tell me the truth." She broke down and told him everything.

Julius invited Meredith to a Bible study hosted by members of his church. She had no concept of what it meant to trust Jesus or have a personal relationship with Him. She didn't really understand what the people there were talking about. But she felt safe and comfortable with them. She sensed these men and women had a peace that was missing from her life.

Alone, after the Bible study, Meredith offered a tentative prayer. "Lord, I don't know what to do here," she said. "But I promise You I won't go back to escorting again. Show me what to do."

A friend of Julius's had heard of Wellspring. He told Meredith about it, but she wasn't sure if it was the right thing for her. She had nearly paid off her car, and she knew she'd lose it if she went to Wellspring. She badly wanted to keep it. It was the only possession she still had.

A couple of days later, she was lying in her bed at night when a disturbing sensation came over her. She felt panicky, as if something terrible was about to happen. In the dark in her bedroom, she could suddenly see a vision of two doors side by side. She understood that one was life, and the other death. She felt God calling her and asking, "Meredith, which door will you choose?"

That night, Meredith made her decision. She would give up the car—she would give up everything—and enter Wellspring.

Those two doors were so clear, she thought. *I'm not going to keep going the way I've been going. I can't. I feel death all around me. I'm choosing life.*

On a cool day in February, Meredith moved into the Wellspring Home. She was nervous, but the welcoming attitude of the coaches and other girls soon put her more at ease.

Meredith wanted to get to know God in a personal way, but she didn't know how. She studied the Scripture verses painted on the wall in her bedroom for a clue. She was in the purple room, the same bedroom that Danielle, the first girl to come to Wellspring, had painted when she was in the home.

The verse on the back of the door, Revelation 3:20, seemed to speak to Meredith just as it had to Danielle. She read it over and over: "Behold, I stand at the door and knock. If anyone hears My voice and opens the door, I will come in to him and dine with him, and he with Me" (NKJV). Each night, she prayed, "Lord, I feel I love You, but something is missing. I don't feel that personal connection. Please come in and help me to know You."

One day about a month later, Meredith sat down in her room to write a letter to the Lord. She wanted to thank Him for allowing her to come to Wellspring. As she wrote, she suddenly felt the presence of God. The words that flowed from her pen quickly filled the page. It was as if God were writing the letter Himself.

Meredith was overwhelmed. *Thank You, Lord!* she prayed. *You've revealed Yourself to me. I truly feel Your presence.*

It was soon after, on a warm Sunday in March, that Meredith and Dixie, one of our volunteer counselors, took a walk in a park near the Wellspring Home. They sat on a bench near a duck pond and talked about God's love for all of His creations, especially His children.

"If you give your life to the Lord, He will take care of you," Dixie said.

Meredith took a deep breath. "I want to do that," she said. "I'm ready."

They prayed, and Meredith invited Christ into her heart for good. She felt excited. She would never be alone again.

Dixie also helped Meredith deal with the anger and bitterness she felt toward her uncle and brother that she'd stored inside for so long. She helped Meredith see how God was healing the pain, and how it had been used to bring her closer to Him. Perhaps most important of all, Dixie explained how forgiveness—though it would be incredibly difficult—would ultimately set Meredith free.

Over the following weeks, Meredith soaked in God's love and Dixie's gentle wisdom. Slowly, the pain subsided. Meredith learned to take all her problems to the Lord in prayer. In the process, she discovered a refreshing new emotion: hope.

Meredith was a new woman when she graduated from Wellspring. Her nightmares were gone. She had forgiven her uncle and brother for the abuse. Best of all, she had found the personal connection with Christ she yearned for.

She was depending on Him the day she revealed the sexual abuse to her family. Meredith spoke to most of her brothers and sisters first, and then her parents. She found herself almost terrified to talk with them about it, but knew it was an important hurdle. That was how she discovered that sexual abuse was a secret that had enslaved her family for generations.

Now the secret was out. Meredith wanted her family to know that with the Lord's help, she was breaking the chain.

The most emotional conversation took place several weeks later, when Meredith, accompanied by her father, confronted her uncle at his apartment in New York. They sat in his living room, Ervin in an easy chair and Meredith and her father on a worn couch. Just being in her uncle's presence again gave Meredith chills, but she was determined to bring closure to the pain in her past.

After a few uneasy pleasantries, Meredith got to the point. "I didn't come here to condemn you," she said, speaking softly and looking her uncle in the eye. "But I was six years old, and you beat me and sexually abused me. I want to know why you hurt me the way you did."

Ervin seemed taken aback. "Don't know what you mean," he muttered after a moment. "That was a long time ago."

Meredith kept talking. She explained what had happened in her life, and the pain and misery that had plagued her since those dark days.

"But now I know the Lord, and He's changed everything for me," Meredith said. "The reason I came here is that I wanted to show you the freedom God has given me. I know He can do that for you too."

By the time Meredith and her father were standing up to leave, Ervin was in tears. "I guess I do remember hitting you a few times," he admitted. "I don't recall that other part. But if…if I did do any of that, I apologize."

The brother who abused Meredith is in prison now. One day, she hopes to have the same conversation with him that she had with her uncle. She wants everyone in her family to find freedom in Christ.

Meredith's current attitude about the abuse in her past might surprise many people.

"People will look back and say, 'I wish I hadn't gone through that,'" she said. "But when I look at where I am now, I say to God, 'If that was part of Your plan for me to get to where I am today, I would not change it or take it back.' I am just so grateful to have the Lord in my life."

Meredith is grateful for another blessing from God. While she was at Wellspring, Julius kept in contact with her and visited when he could. His devotion to her was obvious to all of us—except to Meredith herself.

"You two are gonna get married someday," one of the girls teased after another of Julius's weekend visits.

"Be quiet, Ruthie," Meredith said. "Julius is a very good friend, that's all."

It was a sunny Labor Day weekend when Julius invited Meredith to spend the afternoon with him. By this time she had graduated from the first phase of the program and lived with a volunteer host family.

They took a long walk and enjoyed the first signs of fall— vibrant reds emerging on the maple trees that lined the street, leaves beginning to gather on the sidewalk, two grade-schoolers tossing a football. For Meredith, it would be a season of change in more ways than one.

They talked about Meredith and her experience at

Wellspring, and about the amazing turns both of their lives had taken. Meredith marveled, not for the first time, at how comfortable she was with this man. He was a gift from God.

Julius came to a stop when they reached a school. Meredith glanced around. "This place looks awfully familiar," she said. Her gaze traveled higher, and took in the shape of a sign she'd seen before. Her eyes widened.

"This was Echelon!" she said. "This is where we met!"

Julius smiled. "Do you remember that evening?" he said. "We were two broken people looking to make a whole. Now look what God has done. He had to separate us so He could make us whole people as individuals. We couldn't do it ourselves. But now we are whole, and we're together again."

Julius dropped to one knee, and Meredith held her breath.

"Meredith, I love you and want to share the rest of my life with you," he said. "Will you marry me?"

Meredith was stunned. *Wait a minute, God,* she thought. *I thought You wanted me to go into missions.*

Yet as she looked into the eyes of this devoted, compassionate man, she realized that God had known all along. He had selected Julius for her even before she was born. It was suddenly so clear. How could she ever want anyone or anything else?

A flicker of doubt passed over Julius's face as he watched her face. She had to end the suspense.

"Yes, Julius," she said, her smile broadening by the second. "I will marry you. Yes."

I thought about all of this as I visited with Meredith that warm day at the Waffle House. Meredith was still employing her wonderful skills as a caregiver. She was filling in as a temporary nurse for Alzheimer's patients and helping to care for autistic children. She was also part of a discipleship team at her church and planned to assist Julius with bookings for his comedy business. Both were so pleased that area schools were now hiring him to perform for students.

Of course, an even higher priority than all of that was the little bundle of joy who was currently oblivious to our conversation. *Yes,* I thought, *Meredith is going to have her hands full taking care of many things in the days ahead.*

Yet, now that God was with her, I was certain she could do it. Dixie's words to Meredith had been prophetic. "If you give your life to the Lord, He will take care of you," she'd said. Meredith had only come to realize it recently; He'd been taking care of her from the beginning.

"It is such a blessing to be a part of God's family," she told me, joy lighting up her face. "I pray every day for His will to be done through me. I can see God in every aspect of my life. I just don't know what I'd do without Him."

Neither do I.

4

Lily

A FATHER'S FACE

Six-year-old Lily stirred ever so slightly, her eyes half open, and uttered a contented sigh. She lay in the dark in her bed, her face buried in her pillow. Her little body was just beginning to awaken after a long night's sleep.

A sliver of yellow light appeared under the doorway. Lily smiled in anticipation and pulled her favorite quilt—the blue and white one that Nanny, her father's mother, had made for her—higher on her shoulders.

Daddy was coming.

A knock sounded at the door; it opened. Mason Lawrence was six feet tall, with broad shoulders and styled black hair. An executive at an Atlanta-area utility company, he was dressed this morning in a gray suit and navy-blue tie. Mason crossed the room in two large strides, turned on the lamp on the nightstand, and sat down gently beside his youngest daughter.

"Good morning, sleepy," he said.

"Hi, Daddy," Lily said with a yawn and a grin.

Mason placed a large hand on the back of Lily's head and let it rest there. She liked the warmth of his touch on her dark blond hair.

Mason closed his eyes. "Dear God," he prayed, "please be with Lily today. Give her confidence and concentration at school. Give her favor with her teachers. And please guide and protect her throughout this day. Amen."

Lily sat up and wrapped her arms around her father. This was Mason's favorite part of the day. *Lord, thank You for my daughter,* he silently prayed. *You know how much she means to me. I don't know what I'd do without her. Please keep watch over her—today and always.*

Reluctantly, Mason pried Lily's arms away and stood. "I love you, honey," he said. "Have a good day. I'll see you tonight when I get home."

Nearly every morning of Lily's childhood began this way. She loved hearing her father pray for her; she especially loved the tender expression on his face when he walked in. The twinkle in his brown eyes made life worth living. It made her feel worthy and accepted.

Any child would relish moments like these. But Lily cherished her morning encounters with her father even more because of the "other times"—moments when the expression on Mason's face was far different, when his eyes no longer twinkled.

The "look," as Lily called it, could appear as suddenly as a thunderstorm on a summer day: clenched teeth, pursed lips, wrinkled forehead, angry squinting eyes. It showed up only when Mason was deeply unhappy with someone. It was an expression that conveyed disgust and disapproval. And when it was directed at Lily, it made her want to shrivel up and crawl away.

Lily received the look one day when she was nine. She and her friends wanted easier access to the neighborhood tennis courts, so Lily deliberately threw away the lock on the gate. She knew it was wrong. When her parents found out, her father made her pay for a new lock out of her allowance. Yet the worst part of the punishment, by far, was the expression on his face.

As she grew older, Lily earned the look for other transgressions, such as when she forgot to record automatic teller transactions in the family checkbook.

The first time Lily received her father's sternly disapproving look, however, occurred much earlier, when she was just a little girl. Today, her memory of exactly what happened that day is hazy—except for the moment she blocked out of her mind for years, only to have it return in a dream when she was grown.

She was three years old. She was at a church function. She was in a bathroom. Somehow a grade-school boy had gotten in—she probably forgot to lock the door.

The boy began touching her.

Suddenly the door opened, and her father stood there. What he saw was Lily with her pants down, and the boy standing in front of her, staring.

Lily isn't exactly sure what happened before her father

walked in. What she remembers most is the look on her father's face and the way she felt. She had a strong sense of feeling vulnerable and violated. But even more, when she looked into her father's eyes and saw a shocking combination of anger and disgust, she was sure she'd done something terribly wrong, that she'd disappointed her father in a way that could never be redeemed.

In that instant, she wanted to die.

Afterward, Lily's parents never talked about the incident at the church with her, and she put it out of her conscious mind. Yet throughout her childhood—perhaps because of that terrible moment in the church bathroom—Lily felt a desperate need to win her parents' approval, especially her father's.

But no matter how hard she tried, she never felt fully loved or accepted. There was so much pressure. Her parents had been hippies in their youth but were high achievers as adults, and they had definite expectations of their two daughters.

There was the day in fourth grade when Lily scored 89 on a vocabulary test, just barely falling short of an A. When she told her mom, Lily heard the disappointment in her mother's voice: "We don't make Bs in this family." Lily got the message. Later that year, she cheated for the first time on a test. She was afraid to score anything less than an A.

To please her parents, Lily became a high achiever herself. She earned high marks at school. She competed in sports—soccer, swimming, gymnastics. She was a cheerleader. She sang in choirs. She wanted her parents to be proud of her, yet

Lily

whatever she did never seemed quite enough. She always felt that her family saw her as inadequate.

It didn't help when Lily's grandmother, Nanny, told her she was getting fat. When Lily complained about it to her dad, he defended Nanny, saying that in her grandmother's lexicon it only meant Lily was "healthy." Lily felt hurt and abandoned.

At just two years of age, after a Sunday school class, Lily invited Jesus into her heart. In the years following, she believed in God and understood that she needed Him. Yet in the same way that she felt unworthy of her parents' love and attention, Lily also felt unworthy as a child of God. Subconsciously, she felt a driving need to perform well in order to win His approval.

During her early high school years, that's exactly what Lily did. She went to Bible studies, prayer gatherings, choir practices, and youth leadership meetings. Lily was the picture-perfect Christian teen. But her approach was all wrong—she was trying to work her way into God's grace.

At age fifteen, Lily started dating a guy named Jack. She told him from the beginning of their relationship that she didn't want to have sex until she was married. But Jack didn't want to wait. When he coaxed and pleaded, Lily stood her ground. Then, one terrible summer night in the backseat of Jack's car, he raped her.

Lily was devastated. She was too ashamed to tell her parents. And she felt betrayed by God.

Okay, God, I've always felt not good enough for You, she told Him. *I finally get my life on track, I'm living completely for You, and now this? What's the use?*

Lily began living a double life. To everyone around her she seemed like a happy, responsible, mature Christian girl who continued to record excellent grades at school and was active at church. But on the inside, she was miserable and searching. She drifted in and out of relationships with guys and was sexually active with all of them.

During her college years at Georgia Tech, cracks began to appear in the mask Lily showed the world. She began casually drinking and doing drugs. She took a job as a restaurant manager, and the combined pressure of work and school led to more alcohol and drugs. Lily became a serial dater, yet she never allowed any of her boyfriends to get too close. In her parents' living room, she told her father and mother, "I'm not sure what I believe, but if God wants to talk to me He's going to have to stop doing it through you and others and start doing it Himself. I am tired of trying to believe just because you tell me to believe it."

Lily skipped her Georgia Tech commencement ceremony and went to a friend's wedding instead. There she met Alex, her first boyfriend from middle school. Instantly, old feelings resurfaced; they became a couple again. Lily wasn't concerned when she realized that Alex was an alcoholic as well as a drug user. She was just happy to be with someone who seemed to accept her as she was.

Without realizing it, Lily was getting into a roller coaster that only traveled down. She and Alex partied often, and Lily found herself doing more and more cocaine and Ecstasy.

Lily accepted a position at an investment firm in downtown Atlanta. It was another high achievement for a young woman just out of college, but the pressure was intense. Lily started doing coke during the week so she'd have energy in the evening to get everything done. Then she started selling cocaine so she could afford her increased drug use. The more drugs she did, the more depressed and detached she became. Over a period of three months, she made four trips to hospital emergency rooms to treat kidney infections caused by the drugs.

One day, dressed in a black suit and heels, Lily stood in her twelfth-floor office and stared out the window at the downtown Atlanta skyline. She'd just had a conversation with her boss, but she was so high on coke that she'd already forgotten what he said. *What is happening to me?* she thought. *I can't keep going on like this.*

On another day, Lily slurred her speech so badly at work that a friend had to drive her home. Her boss reprimanded her. Alex confronted her about her drug use; they argued. Lily grew paranoid, believing that someone was hiding in their apartment and planning to kill her.

On a Monday in May after a weekend-long fight with Alex, Lily's sister found her curled up on the couch in her apartment. She was a wreck.

"Anna, I just don't want to live anymore," Lily said through tears. "This world has nothing for me. I don't even see the point."

Lily confessed her confusion to her parents as well. During a Father's Day lunch, she broke down and admitted she'd been drinking, doing cocaine, and selling drugs. She could see the worry and disappointment on their faces.

A few days later, after staying up all night selling and doing drugs at a nearby college, Lily rear-ended a woman on her drive to work. After the accident, she went home. Later that day, she called her boss. They agreed that it was time to part ways.

That August, Lily drove to her parents' home and talked to her mother. She didn't have a job. She was on antidepressant medication. She had cut down on her cocaine use, but she was still selling drugs and piling up credit card debt.

"Mom, I'm so sick of the emptiness," Lily said. "I don't know what to do."

Lily's mother made a few phone calls. Then she drove Lily to her former youth pastor's home. There, they were met by the pastor, three women who had been mentors to Lily when she was a teen, and her dad. They all gathered around Lily, put their hands on her shoulders, and prayed that God would heal her and set her free.

When it came time for Lily's father, Mason, to pray, he nearly broke down. He'd never stopped praying for his daughter since those mornings when she was a little girl, but now it didn't seem to make a difference. He felt helpless. What had happened to Lily? What could he do? Was God still listening?

When they were done, Lily spoke up. "I still don't feel free," she said.

"Whether you feel it or not," the pastor said, "you are."

The pastor's words reminded Mason of the unlimited power of prayer. In that moment, he made up his mind. God *was* listening, and He was still the only answer. Mason would enlist the prayer warrior network at his church to pray for Lily. It was all they could do, yet if the Lord responded it would be more than enough.

Lily's struggles persisted. She continued to live with Alex in their apartment. Their fights grew more frequent and intense. Finally, after Lily went out on her own for a wild night on the town, Alex called her on her cell phone. He was furious. He hurled every insult in the book at her. "You're worthless," he said. "I feel sorry for your parents."

Their relationship was over, and Lily was devastated. She felt helpless and alone. She'd tried to earn the respect and affection of the people who mattered most to her, but all she'd accomplished was to alienate them and turn her life into a disaster. The God who didn't seem to care was all she had left.

Three days later, with little hope but nothing else to do, Lily agreed to meet an old college roommate at a church service in Athens. She was already high on coke when she walked into the church that night with a fresh bag of cocaine tucked into her pants pocket. She found her friend in the back row of the auditorium, then headed for the restroom. Just as she got there, after so many doubts and years of waiting to hear from the Lord, a voice filled her mind: *Go throw that away. I will set you free tonight.*

Lily's heart pounded double-time. God was speaking to her!

As if in a daze, Lily walked back toward where her friend sat. But there were so many people standing in the aisle that her way was blocked. Suddenly, Lily realized what she needed to do. She turned around, retraced her steps, and returned to the restroom. She tossed the bag of cocaine into a toilet, flushed, and left.

This time the path to her seat was clear.

The pastor's message that night focused on the words of the apostle Paul: "Therefore, if anyone is in Christ, he is a new creation; the old has gone, the new has come!" (2 Corinthians 5:17). When Lily heard that verse, her eyes filled with tears. To her, each word was a lifeline.

I get it, Lily thought. *For the first time, I understand what that means. They're all gone—not just my stupid mistakes that have wrecked me, but all the other people's mistakes and sins that have spread all over me and made me feel dirty and worthless. They're gone too!*

When the pastor invited people to come forward for prayer at the end of the service, Lily left her seat and walked down the aisle. Her friend followed. As Lily passed one of the rows, someone waved at her. Lily stopped to look closer. It was Alicia, an old friend she'd gone to church with as a child.

They shared a quick hug before Lily said, "Would you come up and pray with me?"

Both girls followed Lily to the front. They were soon joined by Diane, a young woman Lily had had dinner with a couple of weeks before. All three laid hands on Lily and asked God to bring her peace and healing.

When they were done, Diane leaned in close. "Lily," she said quietly, "the Lord wants you to know that when that guy raped you, His heart broke for you. That was not what He wanted for you."

Lily immediately felt a change in her spirit. She knew that

Diane was right, that God loved her and had not abandoned her that night. Lily was overwhelmed by a new and powerful sensation of freedom.

So that's it! she thought. *When everybody prayed for me a month ago, this is what kept me from feeling free. Lord, I am so sorry for being so angry at You.*

That night Lily told her mother, "I'm ready to go to treatment and get help. If that's what you think I need, I'll go."

Her mother seemed to hold her breath. "Lily," she said, "your dad and I have been praying to hear those words for a long time."

On the recommendation of a family friend, Lily entered a program in Utah. There she spent forty-two days and nights in a desert-like wilderness—and met God.

"I was away from all the distractions, from everything man-made," she said. "All of a sudden I was aware of my Creator and my role in Creation. Everything was so much clearer. It was as if God was cleaning out the wounds of my past."

For part of her time in the desert, Lily fasted and prayed. One morning she felt the Lord telling her, "Lily, I have given you a new name, and that name is Katherine."

Lily had nothing to write with. But she was near a riverbed, so she picked up a stick and wrote her new name over and over in the sand. When she woke up the next morning, with sunlight filtering through a crack in the rock formation above her, the name *Katherine* was still embedded in the bank of the riverbed. To help her remember the moment, Lily picked up a white stone in the shape of a triangle and put it in her backpack.

Only later, when a friend wrote Lily a note, did she discover the verse that has come to mean so much to her: "I will also give him a white stone with a new name written on it, known only to him who receives it" (Revelation 2:17). When Lily's mom told her the meaning of the name *Katherine*— "pure"—it was further confirmation that God was entering Lily's life in a new and exciting way.

After Utah, Lily knew she needed more help to free herself of her drug addiction and begin a new life. She learned of our program at Wellspring and considered enrolling, but felt led to enter a halfway house in Statesboro, Georgia. The secular program there addressed some of Lily's issues, but didn't speak to her spirit. She needed more.

At the same time, the prayer network for Lily was expanding. Her father read a book, *Unrelenting Prayer,* that inspired him to further action. Mason continued to ask for support from the church network, sought the prayers of his morning men's group, and established a team that met specifically to pray for Lily. Her parents also began meeting and praying with a group of couples dealing with "prodigal" children.

Before long, Lily felt led to talk again with Aubrie, our program director. "It's amazing," Aubrie told her. "A couple of months ago, when you were thinking of coming here, our waiting list cleared out as soon as your name came up. Then when you decided on the halfway house, the waiting list filled back up. But now that you're looking at us a second time, the waiting list has cleared again. Apparently, we're supposed to know you. You're supposed to come here."

Lily also learned about our hope to eventually expand

Wellspring into an international ministry. That touched another chord in her heart.

"When I was twelve, I felt a calling to the missions field," Lily said. "But after all those years spent running in the opposite direction, I thought the Lord would never restore that dream to me. Now, though, I believe that God has a bigger plan. His gifts and His call are irrevocable, and I believe that one day I'll be overseas serving Him. And it could very well happen through Wellspring."

At age twenty-three, Lily moved into the Wellspring Home. During our Journey class, Lily connected lines on a piece of paper designed to reveal the "flesh patterns" of her life. When she was done, the picture she'd drawn looked like a huge ball of yarn.

This makes sense! Lily thought. *Now I see why I'm so knotted up all the time. I've spent all these years trying to perform, trying to be perfect. I've been living in the flesh while trying to please God instead of depending totally on Him.*

The seed of Lily's performance-based attitude may have been planted that day when she was only three. It was during a prayer session with one of our live-in coaches and a volunteer counselor that Lily gained a new perspective on what took place all those years before.

"That incident affected my relationship with my dad, my ability to trust others, and my beliefs about my self-worth," Lily told me recently, her voice catching as she spoke. "I thought my dad was angry with me and disappointed in me. But he was angry and disgusted about what he saw, about a violation of my innocence. He wanted to protect me.

"And God was there too. He didn't abandon me. He was confident in His ability to restore me. He told me in that prayer session at the home that I don't have to know exactly everything that happened back then, I don't have to know the intentions of that boy. I just have to know that His grace is sufficient and that He shed His blood for me *and* for that boy. We both need God's forgiveness just as much. It's given me the freedom to forgive him."

As Lily has discovered the deep love that her two fathers—earthly and heavenly—have carried for her throughout her life, it's changed her relationship with them both.

"I'm realizing it's okay to be who I really am, who God made me to be," Lily says. "With my whole family, we're every bit as close as we ever were, but there's a new sense of realness and truth. And especially with my dad, there's freedom."

That new freedom was evident on a night six months after Lily moved into the home. She and two other girls had reached the halfway point of our program, which we always honor with a "Transition Celebration Dinner." Our staff and the three girls' families enjoyed a dinner of spaghetti, salad, and chicken wings in the home of one of our sponsors. Then each girl shared a special memory from their time at Wellspring.

All too soon, it was time for the evening to end. We asked Lily and the other two graduates to sit in a circle in the center of the room. We had the families gather in a circle around them. Then we asked the father of each girl to stand behind his daughter, put his hands on her shoulders, and pray a blessing over her.

When it came Mason's turn to speak, I watched him close his eyes and clasp Lily's shoulders a little tighter. I thought, *So much has changed from the days when this proud father slipped into his little girl's room each morning to pray before heading off to work. And yet—maybe things haven't changed all that much. He's still pouring out his love for his daughter. He's still wishing the best for her. He's still praying for God to guide and protect her.*

"Dear God, each one of the girls we are honoring tonight has been wounded during the battles of life," Mason prayed. "You delivered them to Wellspring to bring healing to those wounds. You are restoring their lives so that they will be equipped to fight on the front lines. I pray that You will continue this work of healing, restoration, and equipping for each of them.

"And Lord, I especially thank You for how far my daughter Lily has come. We have our daughter back. I ask You to keep on blessing her and to guide her in the days ahead. I believe that she has a great future to look forward to, and I ask that she would be used to bring glory to You."

When the prayers were done, I watched Lily and Mason, with tears on their cheeks, come together for a long embrace. There was a twinkle in Mason's eyes, and the expression on his face was one of pure love. I imagined the face of Lily's Father in heaven appearing much the same.

I was sure it was a look Lily would never forget.

5

AN AUDIENCE OF ONE

It was almost 10 p.m.—showtime. Amanda checked her image again in the full-length backstage mirror: long blond tresses, glistening hoop earrings, ruby necklace that matched her lipstick and painted nails, revealing sequined costume. Everything was in place. Satisfied, she threw the mirror one final dazzling smile.

Music began to play in the main room. As always, a tingle of excitement surged through her. She took a last deep breath, then threw back a curtain and strutted to the main stage's runway. Multicolored spotlights stabbed through a smoky haze to warm her body. She couldn't see the crowd sitting in the dark, but the hoots, whistles, and appreciative applause told her they were there. Four hundred pairs of male eyes were focused on her. The feeling was electric.

It was Friday night at The Starr, an elegant "gentlemen's club" in midtown Atlanta, and Amanda was the main attraction.

She was one of the most popular entertainers in the city. She loved being the center of attention, as well as the perks that went along with her glamorous lifestyle. It was hard to complain about VIP treatment, endless compliments, and a six-figure income.

Only in the quiet hours after a performance, when she was alone in her stylish townhouse, did Amanda wonder about the path she'd chosen. Sometimes the pressure to be "perfect" was so intense. And no matter how classy The Starr tried to be, wasn't it still a strip joint? Was taking her clothes off in public really what she'd been put in this world to do?

When these doubts surfaced, however, Amanda quickly pushed them down. *After all,* she thought, *what life could be better than this?*

Amanda's quest for attention began at an early age. When Amanda did something wrong, her mother would have nothing to do with her. Her father was shy and reserved. The result was that Amanda often felt lonely.

Adding to that loneliness was an incident that occurred when Amanda was five. She was at the kitchen table eating lunch, and her younger brother was bugging her. He kept trying to hug her, but Amanda wasn't in the mood. "Don't touch me!" she said. "Leave me alone."

Amanda's mother heard the exchange. "Okay," she announced. "Nobody touch Amanda. Everybody just leave her be."

From Amanda's point of view, the new rule didn't apply

just to the remainder of that day; it seemed to last through the rest of her childhood. Her family rarely hugged her. She never remembered hearing them say *I love you*. Though she couldn't put her desire into words, Amanda longed for affection that never seemed to come her way.

The only affection she did receive, it seemed, was the wrong kind.

When she was four years old, Amanda's parents hired a teenage neighbor boy named Patrick to babysit her. Patrick sang songs to her and brought along children's games for them to play together. To Amanda's parents, he was a perfect choice to safeguard their little daughter.

But on those nights when Amanda's parents were out, after she had washed, changed into her pajamas, and crawled into bed, Patrick insisted on playing another game—a bad, secret game. Amanda hated the game. After it started, she would tell Patrick she didn't want to play anymore. But he always wanted to play again.

Amanda dreaded Patrick's visits. Even when he wasn't around, she was afraid to go to sleep at night. But she was too young to know how to explain what was wrong. Finally, her mother figured out that something about Patrick troubled Amanda. They hired other babysitters.

Yet Amanda's nightmare repeated itself. When she was seven, she was sexually molested by a babysitter while staying at a neighbor's house. It was then that Amanda decided the only person she could trust was herself. If her family couldn't protect her, she would find a way to do it on her own.

Dissociation is a defense mechanism that many children, and particularly intelligent and creative children, employ to deal with trauma. It is a way of disconnecting from pain or abuse in order to survive. For Amanda, it meant asserting her independence and self-reliance. She separated herself emotionally from her biological family and began to see her friends as family.

Amanda further established her independence when she acquired a worker's permit and took a job at a movie theater. She was thirteen. At fourteen, when her mother said she couldn't see her boyfriend, Amanda moved out for a time. At fifteen, she got engaged to her boyfriend. Then Amanda decided she was tired of high school, so she attended summer school for two sessions and graduated a year early. She was not quite seventeen.

Soon after, Amanda broke up with her boyfriend and moved out of her parents' home. Now the separation from her old life wasn't just emotional, but physical. When she landed a job as a waitress at a Hooters restaurant, she was thrilled. She was making it on her own!

Amanda asserted her independence in other ways too. When she was twelve, curiosity and her hunger for attention and acceptance led her into drinking, drugs, and sex. But she had a lot to learn about relationships, as she eventually discovered.

After high school, Amanda dated a man twelve years older than her for several months. She thought they had a wonderful, serious relationship. But when he told her he was getting engaged, she realized he saw her only as a toy. She began dating the manager of a gym, but that romance ended when he said he was gay. For a young woman who relied on others to boost her fragile self-esteem, the failure of two relationships was devastating.

When some of Amanda's friends got jobs as waitresses at a strip club, she decided to join them. She watched the dancers there with envy. They got plenty of attention and earned huge paydays. It made her wonder if she could do it too. *I love to dance. They make so much money. I'm on drugs and miserable anyway. Why not?*

Amanda was a natural. She soon progressed to The Starr, Atlanta's leading adult entertainment club. She added "escort" to her resume and "entertained" men on stylish yachts. The money was fabulous.

On the outside, Amanda became the image of success. She wore a Rolex watch and expensive suits purchased with an American Express gold card. Her townhouse was tastefully furnished by an interior decorator. She drove a Porsche. Four-star restaurants pushed her name to the top of waiting lists. Everyone smiled at her when she walked down the street.

The inside, however, was another matter. Amanda was falling apart. The pressure of performing on stage and in bed, night after night, week after week, was overwhelming. She was addicted to cocaine and alcohol and couldn't sleep at night. She was weak and losing weight. Her dancing style was changing from erotic to embarrassing.

She was losing it.

Finally, after another terrible performance onstage at The

Starr, Amanda realized she couldn't go on. She gave her boss the news: She was quitting.

With the help of a friend of her mother's, Amanda entered a drug rehab clinic. She moved back to her parents' home. She got a job managing a cosmetics line in a department store for fifteen dollars an hour. But she wasn't prepared for the dramatic lifestyle change that would accompany these choices. She was nervous at the store. Compared to her previous income, she had very little spending money.

"Normal" didn't work for her—so Amanda gave up. She started drinking again. Then she had an affair with her manager. Finally, she went back to The Starr, where she danced for the next three years. She became comfortable with the lifestyle again.

But eventually Amanda's troubles returned, this time with a vengeance. The drinking worsened. She got hooked on methamphetamine and started dating her meth dealer, Kevin.

It was a dangerous time in her life. Most of Kevin's friends carried guns. Yet Amanda was often so out of it that she barely gave it a thought. She was steadily slipping into oblivion.

One day, a tiny voice broke through the haze and told Amanda she was on the brink of losing everything. She knew she had to do something, and fast.

So Amanda invited her parents over, and she asked them to bring their pastor with them. It might have seemed a strange request, except that Amanda had always liked having people pray for her. She was baptized as a child and still believed in God. Even now a drawing of a cross hung on the wall of her townhouse, and she had Bible verses written on her mirror. She'd never seen any disconnect between her lifestyle and her faith. As long as she was nice to people, she figured, God wouldn't mind.

When Amanda's parents and the pastor arrived, they were shocked at the sight of her. Amanda seemed barely alive. She was incredibly thin—so thin, in fact, that she'd been suspended again at The Starr. Her eyes were bloodshot and her hair was falling out.

Equally distressing was the scene inside her home. A friend of Kevin's was bleeding on the couch from a gunshot wound in his leg. Amanda didn't tell them he'd just shot and killed another of Kevin's "friends" during a dispute. Upstairs, the atmosphere was like a club. Music blared as young people danced, drank, and took drugs.

Her parents were horrified, but for Amanda, already high on meth herself, it was just another day. "Thanks for coming over," she said. "I'm a little…well, I guess I was hoping you could pray for me."

They did. "Lord, we ask You to intervene immediately in Amanda's life," the pastor prayed. "Protect her, bless her, encourage her, and show her the way to find You. We don't know all the answers, but You do. Shower her with Your love and power."

Amanda passed out in the middle of the prayer. But God had been invited into Amanda's life, and there would be no holding Him back.

At first, the prayer seemed to make Amanda's life worse. A couple of days later, she was arrested and spent a week in jail for accidentally firing her gun and almost hitting her next-door neighbor. When she was released, she learned she'd been evicted and that her neighbor was suing her.

Amanda's mother told her about a program she'd heard of, called Wellspring. "No, Mom, I can't live with other people," Amanda said. "I'm too set in my ways." She drove to a friend's house, hoping to stay temporarily with her. But when Amanda came out to bring in her things half an hour later, she discovered her car had been towed because she'd parked next to a fire hydrant.

Now she had no home *and* no transportation. God was closing in on her. It made Amanda angry. *No, God,* she prayed. *I've gone too far to get better. You're just going to have to let me die.*

Amanda suddenly had the strangest sensation—a strong impression that she was about to lose her leg, that she would be disfigured, that she wouldn't be able to handle it.

She realized it was a warning. It was time to stop running.

"All right," she said with a sigh. "You win, God. I'll go to the home."

~

It wasn't easy for Amanda to come to Wellspring. During her first week, in a class about the condition of our hearts, Amanda had a sudden, overwhelming realization—she had a hard heart. She felt like an ice cube being melted in the sun. She began crying right in the middle of the class.

Then there was her fortress of distrust, which had been built over a lifetime. So many people before Wellspring had tried to help Amanda, but they almost always had hidden motives. I sensed her suspicions. Every time I tried to do something nice for her, she seemed to wonder what I expected in return.

I found that having Amanda at Wellspring wasn't easy for me either. I dearly love every one of the girls who enter our program and want to do all I can to help them. But something about Amanda triggered an extra protectiveness inside me. She seemed so vulnerable. I felt like the little girl I used to be, standing up all over again for my Down's syndrome brother.

At a restaurant shortly after Amanda entered the program, I mentioned to an acquaintance that one of the Wellspring girls had stayed overnight at my house. Without using her name, I briefly described Amanda's background. The woman's eyes widened.

"You let her stay in your *home*?" she asked, her tone heavily laced with disapproval. "What do you say to someone like her?"

I wanted to scream. *Someone "like her,"* I thought, *is someone just like you—a person who has made mistakes and is doing the best she can!* I suddenly felt as if I were with Jesus at the Mount of Olives, listening to the Pharisees who wanted to stone the adulterous woman. Jesus told them, "If any one of you is without sin, let him be the first to throw a stone."

Under similar circumstances, this woman, or me, or any of us might have made the same choices as Amanda. *Are we so judgmental and blind that we don't understand that?* I thought. *Why are we always so eager to throw stones? Amanda needs compassion, not condemnation.*

Perhaps Amanda sensed that condemnation when she

went to bed. Her nights at Wellspring were troubled. She tossed and turned, dreaming about The Starr, dancing to music onstage, and the countless men whose faces all looked the same.

One night, however, Amanda noticed a stranger in her dream. He stood in the back of the room as she danced, his eyes never leaving her, his expression intense. It was as if he could see into her past, present, and future—it was all waiting to be discovered in the depths of those eyes.

She attempted to ignore him, to look away and focus on the audience, but every time she tried his penetrating gaze drew her back. She'd always craved attention, but this man's singular focus was unnerving.

Then Amanda's dream changed. In it, her limbs went limp and her feet froze. She couldn't dance, couldn't move at all. She lost the strength to stand and fell to the floor. Abruptly, the music stopped; the voices and laughter in the audience ended; the lights went out.

Out of the silence and darkness, a single, calm voice called to her. "Amanda," it said. "Amanda, come away with me."

Her instinct was to run. Her legs worked again—she flew off the stage and down a dark hallway, where she ducked into a closet. Cowering in the darkness, the voice still echoed in her ears.

"Amanda, come away with me."

She awoke from the dream breathless.

Amanda didn't mention the dream to anyone. But over the next several days, Laura, one of our live-in coaches, noticed that Amanda was listless and distracted. She waited.

Finally, Amanda cornered Laura and revealed what was bothering her.

The dream reminded Laura of the apostle Paul's conversion experience. In the middle of Paul's zealous efforts to destroy Christians and their faith, he heard the voice of Jesus and was blinded. Three days later, Paul met a man named Ananias, who explained he'd been sent by Jesus so Paul would regain his sight and be filled with the Holy Spirit. From that moment forward, Paul preached about and worshiped the Lord, becoming one of the foremost proponents of the gospel in the history of the church.

"Amanda," Laura said, "I think you might be a little like Paul. You were blind to the sin in your life. Now you're hearing the voice of Jesus, and He's showing you a way out of your misery."

A few days later, Amanda had her own conversion experience. This one didn't involve supernatural voices, but it was just as effective. She woke up in her bedroom at Wellspring. The morning sun filtered through the window above her bed. She threw back the drapes to view our backyard prayer garden, filled with beautiful red roses and a flowering vine climbing up the arbor.

In that instant, Amanda felt she was waking up to a new world. It was as if a black veil had been lifted. For the first time, she understood she was surrounded by people who wanted to help. *I can see it,* she thought. *These people don't have an agenda. They're real.*

That was a turning point for Amanda. When I gave her a new pair of jeans a few days later, her face lit up. The suspicious attitude was gone. For the first time, she trusted me.

"Last night I finally felt a connection was made," I wrote in my journal. "Thank You, Lord, for telling me to buy Amanda a pair of jeans. It was a simple thing that I never would have thought of on my own. It's like You've shown me how to be her friend, and she can accept it. Thank You!"

Amanda began getting up at 5 a.m. every day to pray and read Scripture. She also read nearly fifty books about God. Her goal had changed. Instead of trying to be the center of others' attention, she now focused all of her attention on her Savior.

She'd never felt more fulfilled.

As the weeks passed, I still worried about Amanda. I knew she had a difficult transition ahead, that the temptations and realities of the world outside of Wellspring would prove formidable. But I also saw that for the first time in her life, she'd invited Jesus into the center of her heart. As long as He resided there, I knew she'd be all right.

~

It was almost time to perform. Amanda checked her attire—a black pantsuit with a white knit sweater over it—and took a deep breath. *Lord, I'm so nervous,* she prayed. *Please be with me so that this dance will be honoring to You.*

Amanda was in the dressing room at Atlanta's Philips Arena. She and her eight partners, all young women from the Wellspring program, were about to perform an interpretive dance as part of a women's ministry conference. A crowd of twenty thousand people waited in the auditorium.

The live worship band began to play—that was their cue. Amanda shivered as she joined the rest of the team in the long walk to the circular stage. When the dance began, the huge audience watched every move that Amanda and her partners made. Their faces were displayed on giant video screens above the stage. Soon the enthusiastic crowd was on its feet. But Amanda tried not to pay attention. She was dancing for an audience of One.

With joy in her eyes and grace in every movement, Amanda performed to the music of the contemporary song "Shackles." When the song described breaking chains, Amanda and the other dancers pulled their arms apart. When the song talked about lifting hands in worship, they raised their arms high.

As the final refrain—"Take the shackles off my feet so I can dance…I'm gonna praise You"—echoed through the auditorium, the crowd gave the dancers a thunderous ovation.

Amanda beamed, but she wasn't looking at the audience surrounding her. Her eyes were directed above.

Today, Amanda works at Wellspring, where she teaches classes and assists with the prayer ministry. She says that what she enjoys most is serving as a mentor to the girls and building a "community of friendships." Amanda lives with Skylar, another Wellspring graduate, and keeps in touch with several other girls from the home. They continue to encourage and support one another.

6

Christi

ALL FOR JOY

The petite woman sitting across from me looked as fragile as a porcelain doll. She had blond hair and wore a soft pink blouse and pants. She spoke almost in a whisper, and her hands trembled as we talked. But her appearance was deceiving. Underneath that delicate exterior was a resolve as hard as steel, forged by the unbreakable alloy of a mother's love.

Her name was Sandra. We were meeting in the office of her church. The topic was her twenty-year-old daughter, Christi.

"I just know this isn't my Christi," Sandra said slowly. Tears ran down her cheeks. "I want to find my happy little girl again. I don't know where she's gone, but I want to help her come back."

Sandra began telling Christi's story, and my heart started to melt. Before she was done, tears streaked down my face as well.

Energetic and playful, Christi was practically born with a smile on her face. Sandra still remembers Christi "performing" a song with her older sister, Christi jumping up and down, her dark blond curls bouncing, singing her heart out into a fake microphone. This carefree youngster, growing up in a well-to-do suburb of Atlanta, soon earned the nickname "Smiley." Every move she made seemed marked by joy.

Sandra loved watching her happy-go-lucky daughter, but an unnamed fear always hovered like a lone dark cloud on a sunny day. Christi had been born with a hole in her heart and had undergone heart surgery at age four. Their family had already been torn apart by a divorce the year before; Sandra feared she might lose her baby too. The result, as Christi grew older, was that Sandra and her new husband, David, were protective of their youngest daughter—maybe too protective. They were strict parents, with rules for nearly every situation.

That's how God seemed to Christi too—like a rule maker. She dutifully attended church with her family, often two or three times a week. Christi believed in God and dedicated herself to the Lord at age twelve, but there was no personal connection. The rules got in the way.

Still, Christi enjoyed an almost idyllic childhood. The only time she seemed to shift from her carefree attitude was when she was around her Uncle Randy. She flinched whenever he approached or hugged her.

Once, after a family reunion, Sandy asked her daughter, "Christi, did Uncle Randy ever…touch you in any sort of way?"

Christi

Christi looked away. "No, Mom," she said.

When Christi was thirteen, the rules became too much. She rebelled. She started smoking. When Sandra told her she couldn't go to a Halloween party, Christi went anyway and didn't come back until the next day. Conflicts between mother and daughter happened more frequently and grew more intense. Christi felt a deep anger toward her mother that she couldn't explain.

When she was fifteen, Christi started sleeping with a boyfriend named Jeremy. Not long after, Sandra discovered a note from Jeremy to Christi and realized they were having sex. It confirmed her worst fears. She was losing her baby.

The situation began to spiral out of control. On the advice of a psychiatrist, Sandra decided to let Christi live with Jeremy and his father for a few weeks, hoping that she would tire of the relationship. It didn't work. Then she sent Christi to live with her father.

Christi quickly plunged into despair. She felt abandoned, thrown away. When she talked about committing suicide, her father and stepmother checked her into a mental hospital for a short time. Then she lived with an aunt in Mississippi.

Finally, Sandra enrolled Christi in a program for troubled teens in Shreveport, Louisiana. She told Christi that if she didn't like it, she could come home after two weeks. Christi hated it. When the two weeks passed, she called her mother.

"Hi, Mom, it's Christi," she said. "It's been two weeks. I'm ready to come home."

There was a pause. "I'm sorry, Christi," Sandra said. "You've got to stay there. You need to give the program a chance."

Christi was furious. A month later, she and three other girls ran away to Texas.

Christi didn't see or speak to her family for the next four years. She took a bus back to Georgia and moved in again with Jeremy. She got a job with a pet groomer. On the outside, Christi kept smiling. She gave the impression she had life under control.

On the inside, however, Christi was falling apart. Jeremy was physically and emotionally abusive. Christi felt lonely and empty. She'd used drugs, mostly marijuana, when she was in school. But now she turned to harder drugs, and used them more often, to cover up the pain.

Sandra, meanwhile, was suffering her own private agony. She often woke up in the middle of the night, panicked and worried about Christi. How could she face another day, even another moment, not knowing where her daughter was or what was happening to her?

Sandra and David hired a private investigator to find Christi. They eventually learned that she was back in the Atlanta area. Then one morning, Sandra received a phone call from a police officer. Since Christi was eighteen, he couldn't forcibly bring her home, but he could tell Sandra the address where Christi was at that moment.

Sandra didn't hesitate. As soon as she put the phone down, she looked up directions on her computer, ran to her car, and drove to the address the officer had provided. It was a large apartment complex.

Sandra's hands shook as she searched for door number 107. She finally found it on the bottom level of a three-story building. She hurried up the sidewalk toward the door. It had been so long. What would she say? How would Christi respond?

Then, as clearly as if someone were standing next to her, Sandra heard someone speak. She knew immediately that it was God. "Get back in the car," He said. "Go home. She's not ready."

Sandra froze. She stared at the door, just ten feet away. She'd been trying to find her daughter for almost four years, and she knew Christi was on the other side of that door. How could she walk away now?

Yet God had been faithful to Sandra. On those nights when she'd awakened full of despair and worry, He'd reminded her of the story of Jairus. This father's only daughter was dying, and he'd pleaded with the teacher named Jesus to come and heal her. Then, while they were on their way to her, the terrible news came. "Your daughter is dead," Jairus was told. "Don't bother the teacher anymore."

But Jesus immediately turned Jairus's devastation into hope. "Don't be afraid," He said. "Just believe, and she will be healed." And so she was.

Night after night, Sandra had held on to that story with an iron grip. It was God's comfort to her at a time when she desperately needed it. Would she give up on His love and wisdom now?

Reluctantly, ever so slowly, Sandra turned around. She walked back down the sidewalk, got into her car, and, after a last glance at the apartment complex, drove away. It was one of the hardest things she'd ever done. But she knew it was the right thing. She had to trust God.

And God *was* working on her daughter. Christi began to wish for the support of her family again. She missed her parents, sister, and younger brother. She wanted to come home. But she was plagued by doubts. *I'm such trash,* she thought. *How could Mom forgive me? How could she still love me after what I've done to her?*

Christi confided in her boss at the pet grooming shop. "Christi, your mom will always love you," her boss said. "She'll always be there for you. I know she'll take you back."

That was the nudge Christi needed. When she finally made the call, Sandra was overjoyed. "I'm so happy to hear from you," she said. "I knew you would come back. I'll be there in fifteen minutes."

At age nineteen, Christi moved home again. To everyone, it seemed like a fresh start and a chance for Christi to get her life back together. And at first, it went smoothly.

But the intense anger Christi felt toward her mother soon resurfaced. She was furious about being sent away before. Christi and Sandra began to argue frequently. At the same time, Christi went through multiple boyfriends and jobs. Though she hid it from her family, she also stepped up her drug use. Coming down from the drugs made her even angrier.

The explosion arrived two years later. Christi had been high on crystal methamphetamine for two weeks straight. She'd slept little and eaten even less. She was a walking time bomb.

David found a pipe for the crystal meth in Christi's car. He and Sandra discussed it. They'd suspected Christi's drug use; now it was confirmed. They desperately wanted to help Christi, but they also had her thirteen-year-old brother to think about. Reluctantly, they decided she could not live there any longer.

When they told Christi, she was furious. She lost control. Sandra began packing up her things in her upstairs bedroom, while David stayed with Christi outside so she wouldn't destroy anything in the house. But when David turned away for a moment, Christi locked the front door, ran to the back of the house, and locked that too. Then she ran upstairs to confront her mother.

Sandra had just finished packing a laundry basket full of clothes and books. She couldn't believe it had come to this. She looked around Christi's room. A framed puzzle picture of dolls hung on the wall. There was a bookcase full of Beanie Babies in one corner. The chest of drawers displayed a doll collection—a Scarlett O'Hara figurine, an American Girl "Kirsten" doll in a pioneer dress, a porcelain Southern belle wearing a ball gown. It was a room filled with the typical girlish mementos of a happy childhood.

Yet even as Sandra was packing Christi's things, she had found a glass square with traces of methamphetamine on it. What had happened to the innocent, cheerful daughter she used to know?

Then Christi appeared in the doorway, her beautiful face red with rage.

"You promised you'd never put me out again!" she yelled. "How could you do this to me?"

Sandra took a deep breath. "But Christi, you were doing

drugs here. We can't have you in the house if you're doing drugs."

Christi charged into the room. "Where am I gonna go, Mom? Can you tell me that?" She grabbed Beanie Babies off the bookcase—a fuzzy pink horse, a green puppy, a blue kitten—and hurled them at Sandra. "Why are you doing this to me?" she screamed.

Sandra shook her head. The last thing they needed now was another argument. She picked up the laundry basket and walked toward the door.

That made Christi even angrier—just like always, her mother was abandoning her. She snatched up the heavy porcelain Southern belle and heaved it at Sandra. Her mother had nearly reached the doorway when the doll hit the wall beside her. It bounced off the wall and struck Sandra in the back of the head. She crumpled to the floor. The doll fell beside her and shattered.

Christi stared at her mother, lying motionless on the floor amid the scattered pieces of what had once been a treasured keepsake. In a flash she realized that the doll represented her relationship with her mother, represented her whole life—a messy pile of broken pieces that could never be put back together.

Sandra, meanwhile, lay bleeding and stunned—but not enough to block the love she still felt for her daughter.

I'm not hurt badly, she thought. *If this is what it's going to take to get Christi's attention, if I've got to get hurt in order for her to see that she needs help, then I'm okay.*

The rest of the day was a blur to Christi. In a drug-induced rage, she drove away, then returned. Her mother had been taken away in an ambulance. But Christi was still consumed with anger. She ran over her parents' mailbox, then left skid marks on the lawn. She sped through a neighborhood stop sign. When a policeman stopped her, she tried to escape on foot. After apprehending her, the police found drug paraphernalia in her car. Christi was arrested.

Three days later, released from jail and placed on probation, Christi apologized to her mother. She hadn't meant to hurt her, she said.

But just four months later, Christi failed a drug test and returned to jail. Her life was in shambles. She'd hit bottom.

So had Sandra. She'd tried everything she could think of to help her daughter, and nothing had worked. Where was God? What about His seeming promise to heal her daughter the way He'd healed the daughter of Jairus?

Completely discouraged, Sandra attended a women's Bible study a few days later. When the time came for prayer requests, Sandra poured out her anguish. As the women prayed for Sandra and Christi, a tiny seed of hope was planted in Sandra's heart. That hope grew stronger when one of the women approached Sandra after prayer time. Her daughter had been in the Wellspring program. She urged Sandra to check it out.

A week later I sat in that church office with Sandra. I was deeply moved by the abundant love this mother had for her wayward daughter. I didn't think we had any openings, but I felt in my heart that we could help Christi and that she should be part of our program. Now it was up to her…and to God.

~

Christi sat on her bunk bed and stared at the floor. She was incarcerated with more than fifty women in a "quad" at the Cobb County Detention Center. She wore a navy blue jump-suit that looked like a doctor's scrubs. Her only possessions were four rolls of toilet paper. There was nothing to do and nowhere to go—nothing to distract her from the mess she was in.

God, I don't want to live like this, she thought. *I'm not supposed to be in jail. I'm not that type of person. Why am I here? What do You want from me?*

She picked up one of the inspirational magazines left for the inmates to read and thumbed through it. In the middle of one of the stories was a salvation prayer—an invitation to allow Jesus into a person's heart.

Christi read the prayer.

Then she read it again.

And again.

Okay, God, she thought. *That's what I want. I can't do this anymore by myself. I want You in my heart.*

She waited. Feeling nothing, she was disappointed. Later she called Sandra and explained what she'd done. "Mom," she said, frustrated, "I just don't *feel* it. What do I do?"

"Christi, you don't have to do anything," Sandra said. "Just believe in your heart and receive God in your heart.

You've done it. You might not feel anything immediately, but there will be a change."

As the days passed, Christi started reading the Bible in earnest for the first time. It didn't make that much sense on the first pass. But the more she read, the more she understood.

A court date was set. If Christi would agree to enter a court-approved program, she could be released from jail. Sandra told her about Wellspring. At the time, it meant a commitment of nine months.

"Nine months?" Christi said. "Uh-uh. No. That's okay. I'll find my own way out."

Christi checked into other options—halfway houses, thirty-day rehab centers. Meanwhile, her attorney offered to move her in with a male friend of his, but Christi was leery of that idea. Nothing was working out.

Finally, Christi gave up. She decided to turn the situation over to God. She spent a day fasting and praying. *God, please open the door You want me to take,* she prayed. *And shut any door You don't want open.*

That night, in her bunk in the jail, Christi sensed the Lord speaking to her: "Wellspring will be your home. You will change. You will become who you are supposed to be."

Lying there in the dark, surrounded by a quad full of sleeping inmates, Christi smiled. She had her answer—and a thin thread of hope.

Though she and Sandra were in agreement, the decision still had to be approved by a judge. Then I learned that the judge was a woman I'd met with only a month before to tell about Wellspring. The pieces were falling into place.

On a rainy day in November, Sandra and I met early in the morning at the Cobb County courthouse for Christi's court appearance. It turned out to be a long day. Christi's attorney was late. Then he opposed the idea of Christi entering Wellspring—he thought she didn't need it. Finally, however, he was convinced that this was what Christi wanted. The judge agreed. She was to be released into my custody.

Christi smiled at us as she was led out of the courtroom.

The wait at the jail to pick her up was longer than expected. Sandra, her daughter Erica, and I were still there at seven that evening when Christi finally walked through the door into the waiting area. She laughed—a combination of relief and nervousness—and hugged Sandra and Erica. Then she pulled me into a long embrace.

"Thank you," she said. "Thank you for taking me in. Thank you."

In that moment, I felt Christi's determination. She didn't ever want to come back here. She was ready for a new life.

Christi was nervous in her first days at the Wellspring Home, but also excited. God had sparked a hunger for Him, and she soaked up the teaching like a sponge. She was also so friendly that the other girls weren't quite sure what to make of her. But they soon grew to know her and love her.

Christi's outgoing nature was just part of her personality. But we soon discovered that it served another purpose—it helped her cover up the secrets she didn't want anyone to know about.

Those secrets came out during a "life history" session at Wellspring, where each girl in the program honestly reviews her past beginning with her first memory. For Christi, starting at the age of five or six and continuing until she was about ten, those memories included inappropriate touching—sexual abuse—by her Uncle Randy.

"I tried to block it out, but I know it affected me" Christi said. "I don't want to blame everything I did on that, but it did make me more of a sexual person."

It also, she concedes, likely contributed to—or even was the source of—her deep anger toward her mother. As protective as her parents were, they weren't able to shield her from a little girl's worst nightmare.

And it turned out that Uncle Randy wasn't the only secret. When she was twenty and looking for a way to get off drugs and start over, Christi asked her biological father for help and a place to stay. He sent her to live with a male cousin. That cousin ended up raping her.

Christi had never spoken a word about Uncle Randy or the cousin. The shame, fear, and pain were too great. She doubted anyone would understand or even believe her. For years, she survived by burying her feelings in anger, dysfunctional relationships, and drugs.

Finally, the secrets were out. Finally, God's healing could begin.

It started on New Year's Day during a prayer session at the Wellspring Home. Christi, along with a few of the other girls and Jenny, one of our coaches, sat in a circle on the family room floor and prayed. Suddenly, Jenny turned to Christi and said, "For some reason, I think God wants me to pray for you."

Christi closed her eyes and let Jenny's voice cascade over her like water from a mountain stream. She was barely conscious of the words themselves—but in that moment, she felt the Lord washing her clean. Even as the tears came to her eyes, Christi's heart overflowed with joy. She realized, more than ever before, how much God loved her and wanted to renew her.

Soon after, Christi and one of the coaches met with Sandra and Erica at a local Starbucks. The meeting was difficult. Christi revealed the incidents of sexual abuse at the hands of her uncle and cousin. Sandra was shocked. She'd believed Christi all those years before. Ever since, she hadn't imagined anything improper was going on.

They also talked about Christi's feelings of abandonment and anger. Sandra explained that she wasn't trying to hurt Christi, that her decisions were motivated by love. Through their tears, Christi and Sandra began to see each other from the other's perspective. It was another step toward healing.

Every day at Wellspring deepened Christi's relationship with God. She especially appreciated her time with Jo, one of our class teachers who became Christi's official mentor. In the latter months of the program, she loved hanging out at Jo's house with Jo and her two kids.

I knew Christi was going to be okay when I heard that she had forgiven her uncle for what he'd done, and that she was working on forgiving her cousin. For the first time since she was a little girl, she was free of fear and shame. Her radiant smile was no longer a mask—it was a reflection of the joy in her heart.

Before I knew it, it was time for Christi to leave the Wellspring Home and transition into a "host home," a three-month period of living with another family. I knew she was ready, but I worried about the debts she'd piled up before coming to us. They prevented her from getting a checking account or a car. She needed a job, yet she had little training.

Lord, I prayed, *please help us find a way to get Christi on her feet. Those who will help these girls get a second chance seem so few and far between. You've promised that when we cry out to You, You will remember Your children and answer our prayers. Please give us direction.*

Soon after, I met with a dentist who'd heard about Wellspring. "I really want to do something for your organization," he said. "I'd like to train one of your girls to be a dental assistant. If you think of someone who might be a good candidate, why don't you let me know?"

Immediately, the Lord put Christi on my heart. I drove straight to the home and walked downstairs to her room.

"Christi, I think God has given us an option here," I said. "Would you be interested in becoming a dental assistant?"

Christi didn't hesitate. "Yes!" she said.

Today, Christi is thrilled with her job, and that God picked out a new career for her. "When you came to me that day, it was such a victory moment, just knowing that God cares about me and has plans for me," she recently told me. "It was like He was saying, 'This is for you, what I want you to do, what you'll be good at.' I'd never thought about working with teeth, but I love making people feel better. When you change their smile, it changes their whole attitude toward themselves."

More people than ever are getting the chance to see Christi's smile. I recently invited Christi and Sandra to speak at a mother-daughter retreat I helped coordinate for the church Christi attended growing up. Six hundred women packed a ballroom that afternoon. Many of them were familiar with the struggles Sandra and Christi had gone through. Some had prayed for them for years.

Christi spoke first. She stood on a large stage, where two enormous video monitors displayed her image to the audience. She was nervous, but her words went straight to the hearts of every woman there.

"I used to think that God was all about rules, that He was boring," Christi said. "But He's not boring. He's amazing. He's incredible. He's changed my life completely."

Sandra told the biblical story of Jairus that had meant so much to her, and the words she clung to: "Don't be afraid. Just believe, and she will be healed."

"God has used Wellspring to restore and heal Christi, to give back to us our precious child," Sandra said, fighting tears. "He is so good."

When Sandra finished, she and Christi faced the crowd together, each with an arm around the other. The audience rose to give them a standing ovation. I was so proud of them both.

After the event, one woman after another approached Christi and Sandra to thank them for being there—and to ask for advice. "My daughter is going through the same thing," several said. "What do I do?"

God had healed Christi and her relationship with Sandra. Now He was using them and their example to heal others. The experience made Christi more grateful than ever for God's grace, and for the renewed relationship with her mom.

"She's the best woman in my life," Christi said. "I go to her with my problems and see her all the time. She's my best friend."

The journey has been long and hard. But Sandra says she wouldn't trade it for anything.

"It is all for joy," she said. "I would go through it again if it still brought us to this point. God knew what He had to do to get Christi's attention, to get our attention. It's all for joy."

7

Clarissa

WE'RE ALL DANGEROUS

When I talk about the "dangerous" women of Wellspring—women who have a passion to be dangerous for God—many people assume I mean the young ladies who have completed our program. I definitely do include our graduates in that category, but they are by no means alone.

Wellspring is also a network of staff, coaches, volunteers, board members, and other women and men in our community who desire to stand up for God and make a difference. One way they do that is through the Wellspring Store in Peachtree City. This upscale resale shop supports our program through the sale of donated clothing, furniture, and home decor. But the real power of the store rests in the staff and volunteers who work there. Each has a heart for God and for the young women we try to serve. And like the girls in the program, each has a story to tell.

This is Clarissa's.

The drive home was strangely tense. Clarissa and her husband, Jeff, had just dropped off their fifteen-year-old son at the Atlanta airport. Robert was flying to Duke University for a much-anticipated, two-week summer soccer camp. The trip to the airport had been full of animated conversation with Robert—questions about the camp and his summer plans. But now that Robert was gone, there was suddenly little to say.

From the passenger seat, Clarissa stole a look at Jeff. After twenty-four years of marriage, he was as handsome as ever, with a square jaw and close-cropped, salt-and-pepper hair. He *had* been awfully moody lately. But she'd seen that before, and after all, they were still dealing with the stress of moving. Jeff was a career U.S. Army officer, and when he'd been transferred all over the world, Clarissa had always been there with him. This time was no different, though Jeff had come early to Peachtree City to find a house for their family. She and Robert had arrived two weeks ago.

He's probably just upset about Robert leaving, Clarissa thought. *Once we get settled in, I'm sure he'll be fine.*

As they sped south on Interstate 85, Jeff's cell phone rang. It was Lisa, their real estate agent. Jeff enjoyed photography; she was offering to pick up a new camera lens he'd ordered from a photo shop.

Clarissa felt a surge of irritation. Lisa had called or shown up at the house in Peachtree City several times in the last few days, sometimes for reasons that had nothing to do with their home purchase. Clarissa and Jeff had talked about it. Lisa was attractive and going through a divorce. Jeff had agreed that it would be best for them to distance themselves from Lisa as soon as the sale details were complete.

"You know, I could pick up that lens for you on Monday," Clarissa said.

Jeff's eyes never left the road. Clarissa was surprised by the edge in his voice when he answered, "Do you know where the place is?"

"No," she said. "But whenever we've moved, I've always found out where things are. I'd be happy to figure this one out."

"Just forget it. Lisa's going to take care of it."

They drove in silence the rest of the way.

At their new home, Clarissa changed into work clothes. They'd already unpacked the essentials, and the kitchen was now in good shape. It was time to tackle the living room, which was only half visible behind the remaining stacks of moving boxes. Clarissa had learned over the years to travel light, but every move was still a major project.

She was sitting on a stool, unpacking the first box, when Jeff walked in.

"We have to talk," he said.

Clarissa looked up. What was this about? "Okay," she said.

Jeff took a deep breath, then spoke quickly. "In my life, I want to be passionate and excited about everything I do," he said. He looked out the window. "I'm not passionate nor am I excited about you anymore. I haven't loved you for twenty years. I don't want to be married anymore. This is something you need to think about and decide how you want to handle. I'll be back in a couple days, and you can let me know what you want to do."

Clarissa sat still as a stone. She felt her veins turn to ice. *Did he just say what I think he said?*

She blinked, as if to erase the memory of a bad dream. But it wasn't a dream. Jeff still stood there, waiting for a response.

"I…I don't believe you're saying this to me."

She thought back to a moment in their New York home just a few months earlier, when they'd contemplated the move to Georgia. Jeff had given her a reassuring hug and said, "We've been through these before. This one won't be that tough." That man was her husband, the man she knew and understood. Who was this?

Clarissa found her voice again: "Why don't we work this through? We could see a counselor."

Jeff shook his head. "The only thing a counselor is going to do is make us talk, and I don't want to talk."

Clarissa was stunned. She couldn't think of another word to say.

Jeff waited a few moments. Then he was gone.

~

The terrible surprises didn't end there. Clarissa soon learned that Jeff was seeing Lisa, their real estate agent. Then a couple of weeks later came the next shock: Lisa was pregnant.

When Robert returned from soccer camp and discovered what has happening, he was stunned and angry. Clarissa felt numb. She didn't understand what had happened to her husband. She didn't know why her marriage was crumbling. Suddenly, she was raising a teenager on her own. She didn't know anyone in Peachtree City.

She'd never felt so alone.

But Clarissa did know Someone to confide in. Ever since she was a little girl in Kentucky, she'd believed in God. Now Clarissa leaned on Him like never before. She went to church every chance she got, and prayed daily—sometimes hourly.

Lord, why? she asked. *Why is Jeff doing this? How can he walk away from me and from Robert for someone he barely knows? Is it something I've done? What am I supposed to do now?*

Please, God, this hurts so much. Either bring Jeff back or show me a way to live with this pain, because I don't think I can do it.

The Lord didn't send Clarissa's husband back. Despite her objections, Jeff filed for divorce.

But God did guide Clarissa on a path through her anguish. Though she had trouble meeting people at the large church she was attending, the building itself became a quiet and welcome place of refuge.

Then, on a shopping trip in Peachtree City, Clarissa ran into a friend from years before. Laura was an army wife too, and was stationed in the area. Clarissa finally had someone to talk to. When Laura invited Clarissa to her church, Clarissa started worshiping there and joined one of their Bible study groups.

The pain didn't go away. Every day Clarissa felt the stab of betrayal and humiliation. But God wasn't through working yet.

It was a muggy morning in September, more than two months after Jeff's bombshell, when Clarissa's doorbell rang. The woman standing on her porch looked vaguely familiar.

"Hi, Clarissa," the woman said. "My name is Alice. You may not remember me, but you used to live next door to my sister when you were stationed in Kansas. She heard you'd moved here and suggested I look you up. I live just across the way—we're practically neighbors!"

Clarissa had another friend. Soon she was having lunch with Alice at a restaurant and telling her everything.

"Now I'm looking for a job," Clarissa said. "I don't know how things are going to work out with Jeff, and I have too much time on my hands. I need something useful to do."

Alice patted her hand. "While you're looking, I know just the thing," she said. "You need to volunteer at Wellspring." Alice explained the details about our program for young ladies trying to rebuild their lives, and about the store that helps fund our efforts. She told Clarissa about working at the store since it opened.

"We have the best time there," Alice said. "It's more than a job or a place to volunteer. Everyone supports each other. We're like a little family."

Thank You, Lord, Clarissa thought. *That might be just the place for me.*

On a cloudy afternoon a couple of weeks later, Alice picked Clarissa up and drove her to the store, part of an out-door mall. Clarissa was grateful for the interruption. It had been a hard morning, one filled with thoughts about Jeff.

Alice led her through the store's back door and into a

small room with a table and chairs. She handed Clarissa a blue smock, then filled in a name tag and slapped it on her blouse.

"Now you're official," she said with a grin.

More volunteers arrived. Alice gathered them around the table and introduced Clarissa. Each of the four workers greeted her warmly. Then Alice read aloud a passage from a Max Lucado book that described the sacrifice of Christ for each of His followers: "The cross was heavy, the blood was real, and the price was extravagant…. Call it grace."

Lord, You did sacrifice for me—You gave the ultimate price! Clarissa thought. *Who am I to complain about my problems? Thank You for loving me so much that You would die for me.*

Alice led the group through a brief prayer session, and then followed it with a rundown of everyone's duties for the day. Soon Clarissa was taking a tour of the store. She was surprised by what she saw. First, a beige love seat that appeared brand-new caught her eye. Then she ran her finger along a maple bookcase. *This isn't secondhand stuff,* she thought. *They have high-quality merchandise here.* A few minutes later, she began learning how to take in, categorize, and price incoming donations.

The shift passed quickly. When it was over, Clarissa realized she hadn't thought about Jeff or her problems the entire time.

Sorting through other people's old clothes really isn't my thing, she mused. *But I feel so good! I was productive for an afternoon and did something to help someone else.*

When Alice asked if Clarissa would come back, she said yes.

Clarissa did return the next week—and every week that followed. She began working a regular Wednesday shift. Then in December, when we decided to install a paid "team leader" position for each day, Clarissa officially joined our staff and often filled in on other days.

For Clarissa, her time at the store was rejuvenating. She appreciated each of the volunteers she met. Some were retirees looking for a good cause to support. Others were church members who wanted to reach out to the community. One group of men showed up every Saturday to deliver furniture to the store. Others had been cited for drunk driving violations and needed to fulfill a community service obligation—yet they kept coming back, even after completing their commitment.

Each was there to serve. Yet many, just like Clarissa, also needed healing themselves.

Kendra was a woman in her forties with muscular dystrophy. She was losing the use of her hands and was confined to a wheelchair. Yet every Tuesday afternoon, she arrived ready to help price clothing or contribute however she could. Rebecca, the woman who always worked with Kendra, had her own difficulties. Her daughter was pulling away from her emotionally and refusing to let Rebecca see her granddaughter.

Both of these women had reason to despair, and did occasionally break down during the prayer time that opened every shift. But as Clarissa worked with Kendra and Rebecca and listened to them talk to each other, she consistently observed a simple joy. "Let me get that for you" and "How can I help?" were typical comments. Their attitude was contagious.

Every day at the store was a good day for Clarissa, but

Saturdays were special because that's when girls from the Wellspring Home worked a shift. Clarissa enjoyed getting to know each of them, and seeing the amazing changes they experienced.

Clarissa loved each of the girls in the program, but Donna was a favorite. She was older than most, and the mother of two young children. The other girls nicknamed her "Mama Donna" because she tended to mother them also, insisting they clean up after themselves. She had a warm smile and always spoke a kind word to everyone around her.

When Donna was ending the first phase of the program and preparing to enter the work world, we asked Clarissa to meet individually with her and talk about what to expect. Clarissa and Donna shared their stories; Clarissa learned that Donna's husband battled drug and alcohol addictions, and that Donna had made the difficult decision to separate her children from their father. Before they'd finished talking, both women were in tears.

My situation is horrible, Clarissa thought later, *but maybe God is showing me that other people are dealing with terrible problems too. Donna is so committed to getting her life back on track. She was alone, yet she was willing to walk away from what she knew and put herself completely in God's hands. That takes a huge amount of faith and trust.*

I'm supposed to be helping Donna, but I think she just inspired me more than I helped her. Just seeing her faith and determination gives me more confidence.

I tried to encourage Clarissa as well. I still remembered— who could ever forget?—the shocking moment I discovered my husband was having an affair. I thought my life was over. Little did I know that God would use that nightmare to draw me closer to Him and send me in an exciting new direction. I shared this with Clarissa, and told her that a painful ending can also be a wonderful beginning.

But then, I think Clarissa already knew that. Even though she was dealing with a dreadful ordeal she'd never anticipated, she seemed to instinctively trust the Lord with her future. She knew that her life would one day be okay again. God would somehow take care of her.

Though Clarissa's first year in Georgia was in one way the worst of her life, in other ways it was one of her best. Her spiritual life and relationship with Christ flourished as she focused on Him and the Word. As the weeks passed, her faith deepened as she discovered the blessings she still had, as well as new ones that the Lord provided.

One of those new blessings was a job. Clarissa wasn't the type of person to brag about her abilities, but the truth gradually came out. She'd often handled event planning at Army functions. She had a degree in interior design. She displayed a quiet competence that staff and volunteers at the store soon came to depend on.

In July 2005, about a year after Clarissa arrived in Georgia, we asked her to take over management of the Wellspring store. Thankfully, she said yes. Since then, in no small part due to Clarissa's contributions as manager, the store has grown in productivity and revenue, so much so that we recently opened a second store north of Atlanta in Roswell.

"It's a special place," she says now of the store. "People are there because they want to be there and because they want to serve. Everyone smiles and laughs and goes out of their way to help each other. I'm just fortunate to be a part of it."

With Robert now attending college out of state, Clarissa also feels especially blessed by the friends she's made outside of and through Wellspring. She recently had to schedule a surgery on her foot. Dina, a volunteer at the store, pitched in to drive her to the hospital at 5:15 in the morning. Another friend gave her a ride home that night. Then, while Clarissa recuperated at home, she was showered with freshly cooked meals and phone calls conveying get-well wishes. Dina, meanwhile, returned to drive her to a hair appointment.

"It was so sweet, so giving, for Dina and everyone to do that," Clarissa says. "It meant a lot to me. It's like I have a new family now."

Others feel Clarissa gives back just as much. She doesn't often talk with volunteers about the breakup of her marriage—the divorce was recently finalized—but she will share about her struggles if she feels it might encourage someone else going through hard times. Rebecca, the volunteer whose daughter was distancing herself from her parents, was just one person who benefited from and appreciated Clarissa's compassion.

"I think she's awesome," Alice says of her friend. "The girls and other volunteers love her. She's easy to get along with and nonjudgmental. When I think of the job she's doing after what she's gone through—she's an inspiration to me."

I wholeheartedly agree. She is just the kind of person

who makes Wellspring come alive. With Christ's love in her heart, Clarissa reflects that love to everyone she meets.

Does that make Clarissa a dangerous woman? She laughs at the question and says she never would have said so a couple of years ago. But now…

"I've always believed that little things change the world," she says. "Everything we do makes a difference. Even a smile. Even sorting through other people's old clothes. We're encouraging each other and in small ways trying to help some young women turn their lives around.

"So when I think about it, I would say yes. All those little things add up. We're all dangerous women here."

Clarissa

8

REFINER'S FIRE

Kelly trudged up the stairs to her second-floor apartment and let herself in. Her new boyfriend, Aaron, was at work. It had been a long, exhausting week. Now Kelly was lonely and depressed. She hated being alone.

But then, she wasn't alone. She smiled at the sound of tiny feet scampering on the carpet in her bedroom. Soon two poodles, one black and the other white, emerged.

"Hi, Jack! Hi, Skip!" Kelly said, bending down and throwing her arms around them. "How are my boys tonight?" They returned the greeting with rapid tongue licks all over her face.

To Kelly, the poodles were more than adored pets. She loved them as though they were her children. In her miserable, mixed-up life, they were the only joy she knew.

And now they were hungry! Kelly peeled the lid off a new can of a top-brand dog food, scooped generous portions into two matching bowls, and watched them eagerly devour their dinner. Their enthusiasm brought a smile to her face.

As the evening dragged on, however, the feeling of lone-liness returned. Kelly paced, then grabbed her purse and shook out the contents on the kitchen counter. A pack of cigarettes spilled into view. So did a clear baggie containing a white "rock"—crack cocaine. Kelly stared at it, then sighed. Ever since the first abortion, she'd battled a weakness for drugs. She couldn't seem to stay away from them.

Why not? she thought once again. *At least it'll get me through one more night.*

She lit a cigarette with her lighter, then loaded the cocaine into a glass pipe and lit that too. She sat down on the couch and alternated puffs between the cigarette and pipe. When the cocaine in the pipe ran out, she added more. Then more again.

She lay back and closed her eyes. *I'm so tired—tired of this life,* Kelly thought. *Why do I keep doing this? There's got to be something better.*

Something slippery licked her fingers; Kelly opened her eyes. It was Jack. She stretched out her arm to stroke his head and gently scratch under his ears. Jack wagged his tail in appreciation.

"I love you, Jack," she whispered. But Kelly was too tired this night to dole out more affection. The drugs were kicking in. She'd smoked too much—way too much. She took another puff from her cigarette, blew out the smoke, and closed her eyes again, the cigarette hanging loosely in her right hand. Her mind drifted into a euphoric haze.

Soon she was breathing deeply.

Kelly

A minute later, the cigarette fell from her hand onto the couch.

Sometime during the following few minutes, at the spot where the cigarette lay, a tiny flame sparked to life. Jack barked once.

Kelly didn't hear him.

~

As a girl growing up on Long Island, cigarettes were a form of defiance for Kelly. She knew that her father, a sweet, shy man, and her brother, who was three years older than she, both loved her. Her mother loved her too, she realized, and the feeling was mutual. But as a sensitive girl already dealing with the usual challenges of adolescence, Kelly found Doris Kincaid's parenting style harsh and overbearing.

In some ways, Kelly was a model child. She was popular at school—she was named homecoming queen, she was a cheerleader, she played flute in band and earned varsity letters in track and cross-country. But whatever she did never seemed to be enough for her mother. Doris wanted Kelly to do better, to accomplish more. The pressure made Kelly want to rebel.

There was the day she smoked a cigarette at high school with friends between classes. Kelly was late for her next class, so she forged a teacher's signature on a hall pass. But her mother, a secretary at the school, spotted Kelly on her way to class.

"What are you doing in the hall?" Doris said.

Kelly couldn't think of an answer. Her hands started to shake.

"Why are you so nervous?" Doris said. She leaned in and inhaled the telltale scent of cigarettes.

Without another word, Doris grabbed Kelly by the hair and dragged her into the faculty bathroom. She berated her there for nearly two hours, alternating between insults and questions about why she would do something as stupid as smoking. Kelly felt humiliated. She was grounded from the school prom and denied phone privileges for three months.

In the weeks that followed, Kelly spent most of the time she was at home in her bedroom. She was afraid that if she came out, her mother would start yelling at her. On one of those days, Kelly stared at her image in the mirror. Tears streaked down her face.

"Just wait until you're eighteen," she whispered. "Just wait until you're eighteen."

Graduation from high school was Kelly's chance to escape. She enrolled in a New York state university, then transferred during the next year to a Christian college to be closer to her boyfriend. Brian, her high school sweetheart, attended a nearby men's college.

Kelly spent more and more time with Brian. He was wonderful. She hoped to have a permanent future with him. But what happened next wasn't part of the plan: She got pregnant.

Kelly wanted the baby. She wanted to tell her parents what had happened. She wanted to marry Brian. But when she told him, it was like turning off a light switch. He had no interest in getting married, and he didn't want a baby. Brian began spending more time with his rugby friends and less with Kelly.

Kelly

He said she should get an abortion.

Kelly didn't know what to do. She knew her parents would be angry and disappointed if they found out she was pregnant. She'd be kicked out of the Christian college if her secret got out. Brian wouldn't support her if she had the baby.

She saw no other option.

Kelly was somber as Brian drove her to the clinic. As they pulled into the parking lot, a woman held up a sign that read **You're Going to Hell for This.**

Kelly turned to Brian. "Am I going to go to hell?"

Brian stared out the window. "No."

Kelly walked into the clinic alone. Just before entering the surgery room, a counselor said, "You do know you have a choice, right?"

Kelly's tone was flat. "Yes," she said. But she didn't believe it.

On the drive home with Brian, the whir of the doctor's vacuum still echoed in Kelly's ears. *Oh God,* she thought, *I've made a terrible, terrible mistake.*

She covered her face with her hands and sobbed.

~

After the abortion, Kelly's life took a nosedive. She broke up with Brian and left her Christian college, then reenrolled at the state college. She went out every night. Her evenings became a miserable mixture of alcohol, drugs, and sex—anything to numb the painful feelings of regret and guilt. She fell into deep depression and considered killing herself so she could be with her baby. She became pregnant a second time, and in her bewildered frame of mind saw abortion as the only solution, once again.

One day, on impulse, Kelly slipped into a pet store. A poodle with curly black hair barked and jumped when she stopped to look at him. *He's so cute,* she thought. *He's like me—he needs somebody to love him.* A few minutes later, she walked out of the store with a bag of dog food and Jack. They were a team.

At age twenty-four, Kelly was ready for a fresh start. She packed up Jack and her few belongings and drove to a girlfriend's apartment in Atlanta. There, she found an apartment, a job at IBM, and a new boyfriend.

The boyfriend gave Kelly even more encouragement. He told her that God redeems His followers by giving them a physical object representing His forgiveness. Kelly latched on to that distorted theology with an iron grip. From that moment, she believed God had granted her a special gift— that her poodle contained the soul of the first baby she'd lost.

It gave Kelly a new reason to live. She acquired a second poodle, Skip. In her mind, she had her babies back. Her life was turning around.

But escaping her old lifestyle proved more difficult than Kelly imagined. She and her boyfriend broke up; the next boyfriend introduced her to the drug Ecstasy. Soon Kelly was going to nightclubs and was back in the party scene. She was like a moth being drawn to the flame—despite the danger, she couldn't stay away.

Through all her trials, Kelly had given little thought to her faith. She'd grown up going to church, but what she saw

Kelly

there made God seem like little more than a rule maker. She believed He existed, but she didn't feel as though He had any personal involvement or interest in her life.

Then came the night in her apartment. The overwhelming fatigue. The cocaine overdose. The cigarette burning a hole in her couch.

Kelly's opinion of God was about to change.

~

Kelly blinked, willing the room to come into focus. She was in bed. Her father sat in a chair nearby, reading a magazine. She was surrounded by machines and tubes. Why was she in a hospital?

"Dad?" she said. Her voice was hoarse. She tried to sit up—and pain shot through her legs.

Her father hurried over. "Kelly, just lie still," he said gently. "There was a fire. You have third-degree burns on your legs. You've been here for the last three days."

Three days? The memory of that night in the apartment rushed back: the cigarettes, the crack, the dogs—

"Dad, who's been feeding Jack and Skip?"

Her father looked down and shook his head.

"I'm so sorry, honey," he said. "The dogs didn't make it."

Kelly felt as if she'd been punched in the stomach. *No!* her mind screamed. *Anything but Jack and Skip! I can't lose my babies again. Oh God, no!*

But she knew from the look on her father's face that it was true. The nightmare that was her life had just achieved a new level of torture.

She began to cry.

Kelly would find out in the days to come that she was lucky to be alive. The fire in her apartment had spread quickly, triggering the sprinkler system. If the woman in the room below Kelly hadn't noticed water leaking through her ceiling, help would have arrived too late. As it was, Kelly's heart stopped in the ambulance on the way to the hospital. Paramedics had to use defibrillators to bring her back.

Why Kelly was still alive, she didn't know. Everything was falling apart. She ached for her dogs—her babies. She felt terrible guilt for causing the fire. She couldn't walk for a time because of the burns on her legs. Her parents stayed to help, then left in anger after a fight with Kelly. She broke up with her boyfriend and began attending Alcoholics Anonymous meetings, but had a relapse after two months. A few days later, she tried to buy drugs from a guy on the street. The young man held Kelly prisoner for six hours, raped and beat her, and stole her car.

She met another guy, Dirk, at a club; they became a couple. In part because of his encouragement and in part because she desperately needed a job, she started dancing at strip clubs. Soon after, she and Dirk were arrested for drug possession and spent two nights in jail.

The day after she was released, Kelly woke up alone in Dirk's apartment. Her back ached painfully. She felt physically sick and emotionally devastated. It was her thirty-first birthday.

Kelly crawled into the bathroom, lay on the floor, and

Kelly

began ripping her hair out. It was as if she were trying to tear out every evil thing she'd ever done or that had happened to her. Finally, exhausted, she gave up. She stood and forced herself to look in the mirror.

The woman looking back had once been beautiful, with lively brown eyes, soft auburn hair, and a figure to admire. But this woman's eyes were bloodshot, her hair was unkempt and patchy, and her body, now covered with black-and-blue bruises, was so thin her bones protruded.

What's happened to me? Kelly thought. *I was homecoming queen. Who is this person?*

She answered her own question. "I'm a thirty-one-year-old drug addict. A junkie." It hurt just to say the words.

She turned toward the door, looking for yet another way out, another way to escape the pain. There, on a bookshelf just outside the bathroom door, was a Bible. Without thinking, Kelly opened it. The first words she read were from Psalm 38:

> My guilt overwhelms me—it is a burden too heavy to bear. My wounds fester and stink because of my foolish sins. I am bent over and racked with pain. All day long I walk around filled with grief…I am exhausted and completely crushed. My groans come from an anguished heart. (Vv. 4–8, NLT)

Kelly couldn't believe it—every word seemed to describe her life exactly. She kept reading and reached the end of the psalm:

Do not abandon me, O LORD. Do not stand at a distance, my God. Come quickly to help me, O Lord my savior. (Vv. 21–22, NLT)

Are You really there, God? she thought. *Are You trying to tell me something?*

Whether God was speaking to her or not, Kelly knew she needed help. Without it, she'd end up utterly miserable or perhaps even dead. Maybe, just maybe, God was offering her a shred of hope.

Kelly decided to try. She didn't have any money or health insurance, so she started looking for a halfway house that would take her in. Shortly thereafter, as part of her plea bargain agreement on the drug charges, Kelly was offered the option of attending classes at an area church. She took it.

The women and men she met there were nothing like the people she remembered while growing up in the church. She went to a worship service, and people kept coming up to shake her hand or give her a hug. She felt welcome, even loved.

At the end of the sermon that evening, the pastor invited anyone who needed Christ to pray right where they were sitting and invite Jesus into their hearts. Tears streamed down Kelly's face. She wasn't sure what she was doing, but she prayed exactly that.

Kelly's lifestyle didn't change instantaneously. She still did drugs and went to clubs. But it wasn't the same. She didn't experience the usual temporary pleasure or relief. *I need to just quit,* she thought.

Kelly

Marlene, a woman Kelly had met at church and begun to trust, told her about Wellspring. Then Marlene organized a lunch at the church so Kelly could meet some of the Wellspring girls. They seemed friendly, normal.

Maybe Wellspring is where I'm supposed to be, Kelly thought.

On December 28, I picked Kelly up at the Atlanta airport. She'd gone home for Christmas, which had proven another tension-filled time with her family. Now, after a night at my house, she was about to enter Wellspring.

Lord, I prayed, *Kelly is so shy and seems so vulnerable. Yet she desires to open her heart to You. I ask that You show us how to best minister to her, and guide her into a deep and lasting relationship with You.*

One of the first turning points for Kelly was when a Wellspring coach gently explained that her poodles had never been her children. Kelly wept, but she knew immediately that it was true. Then Cindy, one of the volunteers, led a class for the girls on abortion. During their session, Kelly began crying hysterically. Afterward, Cindy and Kelly retreated to Kelly's room to pray. They asked God to provide names for Kelly's babies, and Kelly sensed an answer: Isaac and Ruthie. It was an important time of healing and closure.

Still, Kelly had questions. *Lord, why was I in that fire?* she prayed. *Why did I have to get burned? Why did my dogs have to die?* She didn't see a purpose for any of it.

Soon after that prayer, Kelly joined some of the girls in a shopping trip to a bookstore. She picked up a small book called *His Princess: Love Letters from Your King.* Since the other girls were still browsing, she sat down at a round table to read. Just as when she'd picked up the Bible and turned to Psalm 38, the first words she read on this night spoke directly to her heart:

> You may not see it now, but you, My princess, will someday be like precious silver that has been refined by fire and purified in My presence. Remember, I did not put you in a fire to burn you out. Trust Me with your troubled heart, and watch Me do wonders for you in the midst of the hottest flames.

Kelly got so excited by what she read that she jumped up and cracked her head on the lamp over the table. She barely noticed the new ache in her forehead; she felt overwhelming joy instead. God was speaking to her again! She read the words a second time, and began to comprehend that the apartment fire had been, in a way, a refining fire. God desired her love that much. He allowed her precious poodles to die, Kelly decided, because she loved them more than she loved Him.

~

After five months in the home, I was thrilled with Kelly's growing passion for God and proud of her progress. But that old spirit of rebellion still had control of a corner of her heart.

We have restrictions for all our girls on who they can see and talk with during their time at Wellspring. We prefer that they focus on God and the program, and not be distracted by

Kelly

anyone who could tempt them to return to bad habits. We had interviewed Dirk, Kelly's boyfriend, and after praying about it felt he belonged on the "no contact" list.

Kelly was unhappy with our decision. She still wanted to see Dirk. She broke the rule and called him; afterward, she felt even angrier with us. Then a girlfriend offered to "help" by telling Kelly she'd give her a ride if she ever wanted to leave Wellspring.

One day, Kelly suddenly decided she'd learned all she was going to learn at the home. She was done. Before anyone knew what was happening, she packed up her belongings and left.

I was devastated when I found out. I knew God had touched Kelly's heart, but I felt there was so much more she had to learn. I feared she wasn't ready to face the world's temptations again.

Dear Lord, please be with Kelly every minute, I prayed. *She's struggling with surrendering to You—she still wants to do things her own way. I ask You to be patient with her and show her the way into Your loving arms.*

A week after leaving Wellspring, Kelly wondered if she'd made the right decision. No one was watching out for her or holding her accountable, certainly not Dirk. He encouraged her to return to the party lifestyle; soon they were doing drugs together again.

Yet this time, Kelly wasn't alone. She knew God was with her and still working in her spirit. This knowledge gave her renewed strength. This time would be different.

Kelly broke up with Dirk. When he started stalking her,

she realized what a mistake he'd been—in fact, what mistakes most of her relationships had been. Rather than lifting her up, they'd been obstacles to her relationship with the Lord.

Kelly began attending two churches regularly, one on Sundays and one on Wednesday nights. She couldn't get enough of God. Then one of the churches announced an upcoming service where members could break "soul ties" with anyone who had controlled them either spiritually, emotionally, or physically. Kelly knew she had to be there.

The lingering sounds of commuters on Atlanta roadways could still be heard outside the church that Wednesday evening. Inside, however, the scene was quiet. Kelly had made a list of every soul tie she wanted to sever. She wanted to break each one individually, so she and a friend retreated to another room and went over the list together. Kelly prayed to break the connection to each person, and to forgive them.

When she was done, Kelly put the list into an envelope and walked into the sanctuary. At the front of the room was a large wooden cross. Kelly picked up a hammer and nail and pounded her list onto the cross. Each blow echoed loudly in the sanctuary. Each blow brought relief. For Kelly, it was a new beginning. She would let Jesus carry her burdens now.

~

I'm amazed today at how God continues to heal Kelly—and to use her for His glory. Laura, one of our in-home coaches, and I recently joined her at another Wednesday night worship service. I could hardly believe what I saw. The shy girl I'd met less than two years before was transformed. She had invited Stormie, a friend and exotic dancer, and at Kelly's encouragement Stormie had brought along a neighbor. Soon, another girl that Kelly had reached out to joined us. After the service, Kelly introduced us to two more young ladies who had opened up to Christ after Kelly invited them to the church.

Kelly checked with everyone to ask if they'd enjoyed the service. Then she addressed Stormie and the other searching members of our group, explaining who I was and how Wellspring had been a refuge. "I used to be in a desperate place," she said. "Then, at Wellspring, I started allowing God to change everything in my life. If you want a radical change, call Mary Frances."

A few minutes later, Kelly walked with Laura and me to our car. "Kelly, this is great. You're like a little missionary out there."

"I know," Kelly said with a grin. "I'm having so much fun!"

I saw the spark in Kelly's eye. Her fire, I realized, was now fueled by a supernatural Source.

Dear God, I prayed, *I am so grateful for what You've done in Kelly's life. Thank You for Your eternal, passionate, burning love for Your children. And thank You for the fire that refines each of us, making us more like You.*

9

Tracy

DARKNESS AND LIGHT

It was so dark.

Tracy had just paid the heavyset woman behind the warehouse door an entrance fee. The small anteroom she'd moved through was almost pitch-black—a string of dim red lights hung from the ceiling, barely illuminating the walls and the door at the back of the room.

A thrilling mixture of excitement and fear surged through Tracy. She stepped forward and opened the new door.

This room, larger and better lit, was filled with wares for sale. Tracy glanced at the items, tools of the trade, but did not linger. She had not come to buy. She walked ahead to yet another door. Now she could hear music. She opened the door, hesitated for just a moment, and stepped onto a platform.

She was in the Chamber.

It was a huge room with a sunken dance floor, disc jockeys on a stage, and a long bar that featured every kind of drink. Loud industrial music thumped with a heavy bass beat. Lights pulsed through a haze of cigarette smoke. And everywhere there were people, two or three hundred of them, mostly young women and men adorned in fanciful costumes. The women wore corsets and dominatrix-style attire, complete with whips and leather boots. The men were dressed as fairies and French maids. They danced frantically, some in pairs or threes, some alone.

The predominant color in the room was *black*.

To Tracy, it was like standing on the fringe of a fantasy world. She felt like Alice in Wonderland, only this "wonderland" was closer to hell than a rabbit hole. It was a place to celebrate evil, a space where the darkness was so complete that it felt pure, even beautiful.

Tracy thought she could lose herself in that darkness. It was, at last, an outward expression of what she'd been feeling inside for so long. She took a final glance at the door behind her, then hurried down steps at the edge of the platform.

In an instant, she joined the throbbing mob of dancers.

~

Tracy was targeted by the powers of darkness even before she was born. She arrived in this world black-and-blue—and not breathing. Doctors had to administer CPR to the tiny newborn while one nurse, a friend of Tracy's mother, prayed fervently.

Later, a doctor speculated that the pain-killing medication they'd given Tracy's mother, Yvonne, might have caused

Tracy's respiratory system to shut down. But Yvonne and her friend believed in another theory. Yvonne had sensed a demonic presence trying to take the life of her baby that day.

There was no sign of demonic attacks in the years that followed. Tracy grew up going to church, and at the age of nine gave her heart to God. For several months afterward, she enjoyed a relationship with the Lord and a strong sense of peace that was rare for someone her age.

Over the next three years, however, Tracy was lured away from her faith. One cause was strife at home. Though Tracy adored her mother, her father was another matter. Jack was unpredictable. He could fly into a rage over the smallest issue, and the rules of the house for Tracy and her older sister changed often. Tracy learned that before she was born, Jack had been angry when he found out his wife was pregnant with a second child. Tracy often wondered if her father even loved her. Most often he acted as though he despised her.

One day when Tracy was fourteen, Yvonne was late coming home. Jack paced, his impatience growing. Finally, he grabbed Tracy and hustled her into the family van. They spent hours driving the streets in the small Florida town where they lived, searching for Yvonne.

It was a hot, sticky night, and the sun was beginning to set. Finally, at a community baseball field complex, they spotted a parked teal Ford Ranger behind one of the ball fields. Tracy remembered seeing it in their neighborhood before. As they drove closer, she spotted her mother in the truck cab with another man.

Tracy sat in the van, dumbfounded. Her mother was her

ally, the only person in the world she trusted. This wasn't possible. "Now you know!" Jack shouted. "Now you know the truth!"

Yvonne moved out soon after that night, leaving Tracy behind with a father who seemed to hate her.

A year later, Tracy was doing the family laundry when the washer overflowed. "What is this?" Jack yelled as water spilled onto the kitchen floor. "It's your fault!" He grabbed a pile of towels and threw them on the floor. "Clean this up now—every drop."

Tracy fell to her knees and started wiping, her back to her dad, but he kept on yelling. He grew angrier with each moment.

Suddenly, Tracy felt something grab her hair and yank her head back. A hand slapped her cheek, hard. Jack was standing over her, breathing heavily, his face red.

Tracy cried in her room until the next morning. She made her decision then—she would never let her father make her feel that way again. No one would. She would stop the pain, no matter what the cost.

Darkness soon closed in on Tracy. She grew depressed. She saw no purpose in her existence. Every morning, she struggled just to get out of bed and face the day. Sometimes when she was alone, she took a knife and cut herself in places where no one could see—her shoulders, her inner thighs. The pain gave her a perverse pleasure, made her feel alive. It was a way to express the darkness she felt inside.

When Tracy was in high school, her mom and dad decided to make another go of their marriage. Yvonne moved back in with the family.

On the day before Valentine's Day in Tracy's junior year, she decided to do something nice for her parents. She stayed home from school and baked a cake for them. But when they got home that evening, Jack and Yvonne paid no attention to the cake. They were angry with Tracy for skipping school.

She had just wanted them to be happy about her gift, but they kept talking about school.

Finally Tracy went to her bedroom. *I'll never do anything right,* she thought.

She'd considered suicide before. She'd drawn pictures of death in her notebook, including a demonic skull riddled with bullet holes. She had written poems about dying, including one she called "Nobody Knows." Now she pulled out the notebook, put on an Isaac Hayes CD, and picked up a box cutter she'd brought home from work.

Tracy's bedroom looked much like any other high school girl's room—pink flowers on the bedspread and wallpaper, a vanity covered with hairbrushes and earrings. To an outsider it would seem bright and cheerful. But to Tracy, it was just another cell in her dark prison. Through her eyes, everything was black.

Just do it, she thought. *End it.* She popped the cutter onto her bare wrist and watched the blood, and her life, drain out.

In that instant—just when it appeared darkness would claim its final victory—an arrow of light pierced the shadows.

Maybe, Tracy suddenly thought, *there is still some hope. Maybe I could get help somehow. I can always die later. Maybe there is something in this life worth living for.*

Tracy blinked. Blood was everywhere—soaking into her bedspread, flooding the pink flowers. She yelled for help. Her shocked parents rushed her to the hospital, where a surgeon repaired the tendons she'd cut in her arm.

Repairing Tracy's soul did not prove as easy. She spent a month in a mental institution, where she was diagnosed as having bipolar disorder. She was put on medications that numbed her. During the next couple of years, she moved out of her parents' home and found work, yet her days remained empty and meaningless.

At age nineteen, Tracy discovered she was pregnant. She felt she had no choice but to have an abortion. It broke her heart. Later that year, at a club in Florida, she accidentally overdosed on a combination of morphine, Ecstasy, and other drugs. For the third time in her life she was on the brink of death, but paramedics revived her.

Once again, the darkness closed in. A black prophecy filled her mind, the idea that she wouldn't live past the age of twenty-six. As time went on, she became more and more convinced that this prophecy was true.

She had no future.

Tracy realized she could no longer cope on her own. She moved back in with her parents, but found little relief. She began to cut herself more often than before, and even willed herself into depression so she would have an excuse to experience the pleasure of cutting. One night at a friend's house, filled with anger and hate for her life, she started cutting and couldn't stop. Before the night was over, she'd cut her arms more than two hundred times.

Tracy accompanied her parents when they moved to Atlanta. It was in that city that Tracy discovered "S and M" (sadomasochism) clubs. The intricate costumes and exotic setting appealed to her creative nature. She'd discovered the "art of darkness." Steadily, like a spider weaving a web around its victim, it drew her in.

Tracy was twenty-three when she thought she might be pregnant again. She was afraid to find out, but after a night of drinking and drugs, she woke up the next morning determined to know one way or the other. She took the test in a Wal-Mart bathroom and waited for the result.

It was positive.

Tracy was devastated. She ran to her car, shut the door, and screamed through tears. *I can't have a baby,* she thought. *I'm not capable of raising a child. But I can't have another abortion—I won't! What am I going to do?*

She went home, then called to tell Mark, the father. Mark was excited. He came over immediately. He even wanted to marry Tracy. But Tracy, balled up and crying on the couch, knew that would be another mistake. Finally, Mark left.

Tracy spent most of that weekend in bed. She couldn't work. She couldn't think. She couldn't possibly become a mother. The dark prophecy entered her thoughts again—she would not live beyond the age of twenty-six. She couldn't get it out of her mind.

She was down to her last hope.

God, she prayed slowly, *if You are there, if You are real and can hear this, I need help here. I can't have another abortion. I don't see how I can raise a child, either, but if that's what You want…Your will be done.*

Three weeks later, Tracy had a miscarriage. It was awful, but in another sense a relief.

In the following weeks, Tracy continued visiting clubs and doing drugs. But the prayer she'd uttered in desperation proved the beginning of a conversation with God. She found herself talking to Him occasionally. It was nothing elaborate, just simple statements such as "I need You" or "Show me the way." She didn't really expect an answer.

Then, on a day in June, the strangest desire came over Tracy. She thought, *I want to go to church.*

She told Yvonne, who promised to take her that weekend. On Sunday morning, after another Saturday night at the Chamber, Tracy and her mother drove to a church Yvonne had visited once before. The line to get in stretched onto the sidewalk. The church, they learned, was putting on a play called "Eternity." It was sold out, but there would be three more performances that day.

Tracy wasn't sure why, but she felt keenly disappointed. She and Yvonne decided to come back for the second performance. That one was sold out too—as was the third.

Finally, on their fourth visit that day, Tracy and Yvonne were able to make it inside the church to see the play's last showing. To Tracy, the play was a wake-up call. The message was about knowing where you would spend eternity—heaven or hell—and what that would be like. As Tracy thought about her life so far, she realized she had a pretty good idea which way she was headed.

After the play, the pastor invited anyone in the audience who wanted to give their life to God to come forward. *If this* is reality, Tracy thought, *I need to be down there.* She stood and, along with many others in the crowd, walked to the front. One of the performers in the play—an angel still wearing her wings and halo—sat down with Tracy on the steps to pray with her.

A few minutes later, Tracy rededicated her life to God.

Many people believe that when they become Christians, their problems will melt away like an ice cube in sunshine. But often it does not work that way at all. For Tracy, it was as if the darkness that had encircled her for years now took on a physical presence. She could almost see heavy black tentacles reaching out of the shadows to grab and hold her.

Tracy began reading the Bible and other books about God. She was so hungry to learn more. She went back to church. She was on the floor every day, crying out to God in worship. But the darkness did not want to let her go. She felt as if hell were being born for the first time, unleashing all its demons specifically to torment her. Buried emotions broke loose inside her—anger and hate.

Her body and soul proved a battleground between dark and light. She felt an incredible pressure, as if everything were being squeezed out of her. She doubted that anything would be left by the time the war was over.

One afternoon, as she sat alone in a Wendy's parking lot, the pressure became too much. Tracy pulled a knife out of her purse. She turned it around and around in her hand, watching the sun reflect off the silver blade. She hated herself and her life. She didn't see how it would get better. She was sick of trying to hide the pain.

Using the rearview mirror as a guide, Tracy began cutting her face in symmetrical patterns. It was art with blood—the art of darkness. When she was done, she called her mother, who met her there and rushed her to a hospital. One nurse burst into tears when she saw Tracy.

Tracy spent more time in a mental institution. Yvonne prayed desperately for her daughter. She wanted to help, but didn't know what to do. Both realized that something drastic needed to happen.

At church, Tracy spoke with a woman who had tried to mentor her in the past. The woman mentioned Wellspring, and then encouraged Tracy to talk to Christiana, a member of our staff who attended the same church. Tracy was skeptical, but when she met with Christiana and found out more about the program, she became both scared and excited about the idea. Was this a way out of the darkness?

Tracy needed an answer from God. She prayed and fasted for three days, but felt no closer to knowing what to do. Finally, while sitting in church that Sunday, she received a strong impression she was sure came from the Lord: She was to go to Wellspring.

Soon after, Tracy met Christiana at a Starbucks. "I've been praying about this," Christiana said. "I believe God wants you to go off your meds cold turkey and come to Wellspring right now. Are you willing to do that?"

Tracy swallowed. She was scared, but this was exactly what her heart was telling her too. "Yes," she said.

In that moment, Tracy believes, something supernatural took place. God had shown her the way to the Light. He was offering His hand. When she took it by saying yes, it was as if the heavy black tentacles that had been clawing at her fell away. Now it was just her and God.

The night before she moved into the Wellspring Home, Tracy was so nervous she slept with her Bible. She needed something tangible to hold on to. She'd quit her job as manager of a retail store and left behind the only life she knew, crazy as it was. Yet she felt at peace about her decision. If this was what God wanted, she was determined to give it everything she had.

In the home, Tracy was timid at first, but she connected well with the staff and other girls. Though she itched and had trouble sleeping during the first two weeks, she had remarkably few side effects from dropping her medications. She still battled depression, but began learning how to take those feelings to God and let Him bring peace into her heart.

Tracy's passion for God grew. The light was winning the war inside her, crowding out the darkness. Yet even now, the darkness didn't quit. It wanted her back.

There were things Tracy didn't understand. *God, You knew we would go through all this suffering and pain and wretchedness,* she prayed. *So why did You create us?* It didn't make sense to her. Sometimes she grew frustrated. And like a creeping black fog, the darkness took advantage of her frustration to once again invade her heart.

It was a Saturday night, about seven months after Tracy had entered Wellspring. She'd already completed the first part of the program; now she lived with a host family and had more freedom. She was struggling; the darkness pulled at her.

Before she knew it, Tracy found herself driving through Atlanta toward a familiar neighborhood. Nothing had changed—the unmarked warehouse, the dim anteroom, the merchandise store. And suddenly, there she was, back in evil's wonderland.

"Tracy!" a woman dressed in black leather screamed. "You're back!" Old friends crowded around, greeting her enthusiastically. She was excited to see them.

Yet it wasn't the same. Tracy felt awkward standing on the dance floor in the middle of this dark fantasy world. She enjoyed talking with her friends, but when she left, she felt empty. She didn't belong there anymore.

Tracy actually cried that night. It was hard to let go of the attraction to that world. But she knew there was a better place for her—a place of true beauty and light. She read and reread a Bible passage that seemed to speak only to her: "Listen, O daughter, consider and give ear: Forget your people and your father's house. The king is enthralled by your beauty; honor him, for he is your lord" (Psalm 45:10–11).

Tracy's struggle didn't end there. For weeks after that night, she called me each Saturday to ask for prayer. I believe God intervened through those prayers, helping Tracy realize she must never again return to places of darkness. Only by consistently focusing on and honoring Him would she be free of evil's grip.

Today, Tracy *is* free, and she has joined the fight on the side of beauty and light. She helped organize a book group with some of the girls at her church. She has substituted for the coaches at Wellspring when we've needed a hand. She's become a resource for girls in the program, especially those that have recently stumbled. They view Tracy as a safe harbor, someone who will say "I love you" no matter what.

Tracy has seen darkness and light. More than most, she understands the continuing battle between them, and what is at stake in the war. She is a warrior for the forces of Good.

I recently had the pleasure of celebrating a victory in that battle. I joined Tracy and about twenty other Wellspring graduates, staff, and volunteers at a restaurant to honor her. It was a very special occasion: her twenty-seventh birthday.

Each of us brought a rose and a card to give to Tracy. One by one, we handed them to her and explained to the group how she had been a sweet fragrance in our lives. Tracy beamed through it all. Finally, it was her turn to speak.

"I've never celebrated my birthday much," she said quietly. "I didn't understand why I should celebrate my life when I despised the day of my birth. But over the last few years, God has been changing my perspective. This morning, as I was driving, a light came on. I said, 'Lord, this is a day of victory. Satan has been trying to claim me since the day I was born. But here I am, alive, with many more vibrant years ahead of me.' So…praise God!"

As Tracy spoke, surrounded by the warm embrace of friends, I saw her excited smile deepen. I was struck by her appearance. Her face glowed like a beacon.

This *was* a day to celebrate. Tracy's countenance—and her very life—was a portrait of light shining through darkness. I leaned back in my seat and returned Tracy's grin.

This, I thought, *is truly beautiful.*

10

REDEEMING LOVE

There is no love story quite like the biblical account of Hosea and Gomer. At the Lord's instruction and with His blessing, the prophet Hosea marries an unfaithful woman named Gomer. He loves her deeply. Together they build a life and have three children. Yet their bliss does not last. Gomer breaks her husband's heart by running away to again "chase after her lovers" (Hosea 2:7).

It is a tragic and familiar story, but with an unfamiliar twist: God instructs Hosea to "show your love to your wife again" (Hosea 3:1), and Hosea obeys. When Hosea discovers that Gomer has fallen into slavery, he buys her back.

I can just imagine the look on Gomer's face when Hosea handed over the silver and barley to set her free. *Why is he doing this?* she must have thought. *He can't still love me, not after what I've done to him. I don't deserve this!*

It is a picture of the love we all seek, but cannot quite

believe—God's enduring, redeeming love for each of us.

The girls who go through the Wellspring program are desperately searching for this love. Yet so are the rest of us who try to help them. Ava, one of our coaches and program directors, recently discovered for herself just how wide and deep is the incredible, eternal, redeeming love of our Lord.

~

The unbidden image suddenly filled her mind—a skull resting atop white bones arranged in a well-known shape: a skeleton.

Ava shivered and opened her eyes. She was on her knees in her dorm room at a small liberal arts college in Georgia. A Bible lay on the floor in front of her. She'd been praying, asking the Lord for guidance about her relationship with her fiancé. *But what*, she wondered, *did a skeleton have to do with Steve?*

Ava and Steve had been a couple almost from the day they'd met six years ago as staff members at a summer camp. They'd grown up together. Each seemed to know instinctively what the other was thinking. It was, everyone said, a match made in heaven.

Except that in the last few months, something had changed. Ava couldn't put it into words, but she felt something about their relationship wasn't right. Steve seemed distant. After classes, he spent more and more time working on his new interest, acting, and less and less with Ava.

As she thought about the image of the skeleton, Ava's mind flashed to a Scripture she'd read recently on a disciple-

Ava

ship retreat. The words of Jesus in Matthew 23:27 were still fresh in her mind: "Woe to you, teachers of the law and Pharisees, you hypocrites! You are like whitewashed tombs, which look beautiful on the outside but on the inside are full of dead men's bones and everything unclean."

Lord, what are You telling me? she prayed. *Is that what my relationship with Steve is like—alive and beautiful on the outside, but on the inside full of dead men's bones?*

The more she prayed about it, the more Ava realized it was true. She'd dreamed of being a wife and mother since she was a little girl. As a child, she'd played almost exclusively with baby dolls, always imagining the day she would have a husband and raise a family. But she had tried to mold Steve into the man of her dreams without paying attention to what was happening between them. As much as she cared for him, there was something hollow, an emptiness, at the core of their relationship.

Slowly, reluctantly, she faced the truth: She needed to end the relationship. She could hardly bear the thought, yet she realized God had something else in mind for both of them.

Soon after, sitting on the bed in her room, Ava tried to explain her feelings to Steve. She read the passage from Matthew and an entry from her journal to him.

At first Steve didn't get it. He thought Ava meant only to postpone their engagement.

"You don't understand," Ava said, fighting to keep her emotions in check. "I'm not yours. I can't do this. These last six years with you have meant so much to me, but I'm sure now that God is calling me to a different life."

Steve was more stunned than angry. They talked more. Finally, he got up to leave.

"I don't want you to go," Ava said. "When you walk out that door, everything is going to change. Everything."

Ava was right. For her, the breakup was incredibly painful, emotionally and physically. She felt as if she'd lost everything. She couldn't sleep. She couldn't eat, and lost thirty pounds. She'd been with Steve so long that it seemed as if half of her was missing. She even called an old friend to ask what things she'd liked before she met Steve. She couldn't remember the person she used to be.

With no one else to turn to, Ava spent more and more time with God in prayer. Her pleas took on a desperate tone. *Lord, what happened to Steve and me?* she prayed. *Please fix whatever the problem is and bring us back together. I don't know how I can go on like this.*

At twenty-one years old, Ava was confronting her heart's desire—an overpowering need to love and be loved. She thought that human affection, the love of a man, would satisfy her longing. But the Lord was about to reveal a more fulfilling answer.

God didn't "fix" Ava's relationship with Steve. The hole in her heart remained. But through her pain and her prayers, Ava noticed a strange thing happening. The love she'd focused for years on Steve now began to pour out of her like a runaway river toward the Author of love. It unleashed a passion for God that she had never known. Even if she'd wanted to, Ava could not have held it back. She prayed, thought about God, and talked with Him nearly constantly. When she wrote in her journal, her entries became love letters to the Lord.

"God, I have given You so much of my pain, confusion, hurt, fear, heartbreak, loneliness, anguish, and tears in the past months," she wrote. "I have shared them all with You, and You have taken them and helped me carry the load. Thank You for that! Now I want to share the good things You've given me. I want to share the joy, excitement, love, contentment, laughter, and smiles. I want to give all that to You as my praise offering. I want more of You!"

The change inside Ava began to show on the outside. She started eating and sleeping normally again. Her face reflected a newfound serenity.

One night in Ava's dorm room, her phone rang. It was Sally, a friend who'd recently become engaged herself.

"Ava," she said through tears, "can I come over?"

A few minutes later, Sally and Ava were sitting together on Ava's floor. "I can't tell you what it is," Sally said, "but would you pray for me?"

Sally seemed to feel better after the prayer.

"You know, Ava," she said, "I look at your life right now, and even though you're going through all this stuff, you're so at peace. I want what you have. I just want to be around you so your passion for God is something I can have too."

Sally's comments blew Ava away. She'd grown up in church and always believed in God. But now, for the first time, Ava understood that God was all He said He was. Even other people could see what was happening to her. He was taking her to a new level of intimacy.

Lord, I see it! she prayed. *You will speak to me and guide me and draw near to me if only I will draw near to You. Thank You for showing me. Thank You for changing my life!*

Ava soon found herself changing in other ways. She'd always been athletic—she played varsity basketball in high school—and never thought of herself as a "girly girl." Yet as her relationship with God deepened, she discovered a desire to understand what it meant to be a godly woman, and to share that knowledge with others. Even though she was carrying eighteen hours in her last semester of college, she read book after book about women of faith. Then she started a Bible study for freshman girls that explored the role of women in God's family.

Ava would graduate at the end of December with a degree in English. She planned to either work toward a master's degree and accept a job as a nanny or go abroad and teach English. Then her older sister told Ava that a ministry for young women, called Wellspring Living, had an opening. Ava soon contacted me, and I was immediately impressed by her enthusiasm and desire to play a role in leading girls to God. I offered her a position.

But Ava wasn't ready to commit. So many times in her life, she had made decisions without waiting on the Lord's guidance. This time she wanted to be sure.

Ava prayed. She read Scripture. Still she didn't sense an answer.

A few days later, near five o'clock on a Friday, she arrived at my office. "I'm so sorry, Mary Frances," she said. "I know you deserve a decision. I just don't feel I've heard from God on what I should do, so I'm going to have to say no."

I understood, even though I was disappointed. I thought she seemed disappointed too. "Ava," I said, "if you change your mind, you can call me anytime."

That evening, at her mother's house, Ava finished reading a novel called *Redeeming Love*. It was a story about a nineteenth-century prostitute who continuously runs away from the unconditional love of God and of a godly man. Finally, at the end of the story, the woman stops running. She gives her life to the Lord and her heart to the man who can't live without her. And every year thereafter, she spends time with young prostitutes, encouraging them to turn their lives over to God.

When Ava finished the book, she put it down and closed her eyes. *God, what are You trying to tell me here?* she prayed. *Are You messing with me? Does this mean I should go to Wellspring?*

Ava didn't hear an answer. Restless, she pulled a sweatshirt on over her T-shirt and sweats and went for a walk.

The night was cool and dark. Ava headed for a wooded area at the end of the neighborhood. Soon, she found herself on a dirt path she'd never explored before. She followed it into a grove of trees. She couldn't see where it led; the only light came from the stars shining overhead.

God, give me a picture of what You want, she prayed. *I only want to be obedient.*

She walked a long way, then stopped. The uncertainty was driving her crazy. She wanted to do the right thing. She wanted to follow His lead. Why was the Lord so silent?

In the darkness, she dropped to her knees. *God, please give me a picture,* she prayed again. *Whatever it is, I'll be obedient.* The only answer she heard was a breeze moving through the trees.

Finally, with a heavy heart, Ava got up and began walking again.

It was barely a minute later that she heard it—the faint sound of running water, coming from somewhere ahead.

Ava's heart beat faster. She hurried forward in the dark, still taking care to keep to the path. She followed it around a bend, and the sound of rushing water grew louder. Then, through a gap in the trees, barely visible in the starlight, she saw it.

It was a creek. A spring.

Ava laughed and almost ran along the path to the point where it connected to the stream. It was only a small creek. She'd never seen or heard of one in this area. But God had known it was here all along.

Ava stepped lightly on a rock near the edge of the creek to reach a larger rock in the middle of the stream. She knelt and dropped her hands into the cool water. She shivered, but not because of the temperature of the creek.

"God, thank You!" she cried. "Thank You for showing me that Wellspring is Your choice for me. I want to be Yours. I want to be wholly devoted to You. I will do this."

Less than forty-five minutes later, a breathless Ava was sitting in my basement. "Mary Frances, I know it's late, and I know this is a crazy thing to say," she said. "But I told you no a few hours ago, and now I'm here to tell you yes."

I breathed my own silent prayer of thanks. "Ava, I don't think it's crazy at all."

Ava started at Wellspring in January. The first two weeks were something of a shock to a young lady who'd grown up in the church and always been a "good girl." As a coach-in-training, Ava believed that she needed to be in control, to show the other girls she had everything together. But the reality of the evil each girl in the home faced was overwhelming.

One night, a girl in the program named Elaine told about allowing herself to be gang-raped so she could get drugs. She experienced so much shame and guilt while telling the story that she threw up.

Ava kept her cool while her training coach comforted Elaine. But as soon as the situation was taken care of, she ran downstairs to our prayer closet, shut the door, and buried her head in a pile of pillows.

"God, I know You called me here, but You've make a mistake!" she said. "I'm Miss Vanilla. I have nothing to give these girls, no experience, no wisdom. What am I doing here?"

Suddenly, the image of a burning bush appeared in Ava's mind. She got up, picked up the Bible that we keep in the prayer closet, and turned to the account of Moses and the burning bush in Exodus 3. She read of God's command to Moses to free His people, and the excuses Moses gave as to why God should choose someone else.

Ava sat up straighter as she reread God's answer to Moses in verse 12: "I will be with you."

She realized what the Lord was saying to Moses—and to her. *God, I understand,* she prayed. *You're saying it doesn't mat-*

ter if I've fallen short, if I can't speak well, what my past is. You have chosen to let me join in what You're doing to bring freedom to the captives. This is about You, and You want me to be part of it.

Ava felt as if the heavy pressure pushing her down had suddenly been lifted. True, she didn't have experience or training for helping the young women of Wellspring. Yet she now believed that if God had called her, He would also equip her.

As the girls in the program devoted more and more time to learning about God and His Word, Ava joined them. She found herself depending on Him not just day by day, but moment by moment. It changed her focus from inward to outward.

For the first time in her life, Ava began developing friendships that weren't based on what the other person could give back. She was strict with the Wellspring girls at times, but her toughness was born out of a genuine love for each of them.

Ava tried to explain that love to two of the girls during their Sunday night chapel time. Both Elyse and Bonnie had struggled with making wise choices. Elyse had been involved in one bad relationship after another. Bonnie couldn't seem to say no to drugs. Ava had talked many times with both about making better decisions.

In the living room of the home, Ava read from the book of Nehemiah about the rebuilding of the walls of Jerusalem. She told how men armed with spears, shields, bows, and arrows stood ready to protect the workers and the city from enemies while other men worked to restore the walls.

"You guys are like the people of Israel," Ava said. "You're

both working hard to rebuild your lives, stone on top of stone, while the enemy tries to attack you. By our prayers and words from Scripture and just being here, we are fighting for you. We love you. We're giving you this part of our lives so you can rebuild yours."

Elyse began to cry. "You believe in me enough to be here," she said through tears. "Thank you."

That night was a revelation for Ava. She saw that even though she hadn't been through the same experiences as most of the other girls in the program, she did understand their pain and loneliness. Like them, she'd been distant from God. They all needed the same compassion, the same forgiveness, the same love.

As Ava worked with the girls and their problems, she continued to rely on the Lord for solutions. Her Father in heaven became her consistent and faithful companion. When she read about God's words to Gomer in the book of Hosea, she felt as if He were speaking to her alone: "I will lead her into the desert and speak tenderly to her." She responded to His tenderness with love.

There were still times when Ava also wished for the tender touch of a man. She occasionally went to events sponsored by a church singles group, but she felt awkward and out of place. Some days she came home and cried afterward. Yet through her new and intimate relationship with the Lord, Ava felt more fulfilled than ever before. Though she still had a desire to be a wife and mother, she saw for the first time that God might have another plan for her life, and she accepted it.

God, my greatest desire is for You, she prayed. *My heart is satisfied in You. Though I still hope to be blessed someday with a husband, I want most of all to abide in You. Please fill me with the knowledge of Your perfect will. I love You and trust my future to You.*

It was a cool, cloudy evening in 2005 when Ava attended a Christmas party for the church singles group. At a long table at the restaurant, she sat across from Perry, a newcomer. Perry was tall, with dark hair and an easy smile. Like Ava, he enjoyed outdoor adventures such as rock climbing and spelunking.

It wasn't long before Perry and Ava were spending time together. Yet both were careful to keep the relationship at a "friends only" level. Like Ava, Perry had been in relationships that ended painfully. Each of their desire was to please God above everything else.

When the friendship deepened, however, Ava began asking the Lord if Perry was the man He'd chosen for her. She sensed His approval to begin a serious dating relationship.

A few weeks later, Ava and Perry sat on a couch and talked into the night at her mother's house. They'd never spoken of their deepest feelings for each other. They'd promised not to say anything unless they were sure, unless there was genuine commitment behind the words.

During a pause in the conversation, a strange look came over Perry's face. He swallowed hard, then blurted out, "I love you!"

Before Ava could respond, Perry jumped up and went into the kitchen. She could hear him getting a drink of water.

She knew he was stalling. Finally, he came back and sat down.

Perry took a deep breath. "Okay," he said. "I really need to know how you feel about what I just said."

Ava smiled and took Perry's hand. "I knew it already," she told him. "I knew that you love me because you open the door for me and get mad if I open it myself. I knew because you bring your coat to me from across the room when you see I'm cold. I knew because you make such an effort to get to know my family, because you know how important that is to me. I knew because you put up boundaries for our physical relationship and kept to them because you care about our integrity and our relationship with God. You've shown me you love me for a long time."

It was a warm evening in July when Perry brought Ava to a shimmering lake and led her to a boat dock lined with flickering white candles. A private dinner of his favorite entree, ravioli and meatballs, and her favorite dessert, cookies and cream ice cream, awaited them.

Perry had something else to take care of before dinner, however. The sun had just begun to fall behind trees on the far side of the lake when he walked Ava onto the dock and held her there for a brief dance. Their only background music was the sound of water gently lapping against the pilings. Then Perry spun Ava around and dropped to one knee.

Her heart skipped a beat. She knew what was coming.

"Ava," he said, looking up at her, "will you be my wife?"

Of course, she answered yes. She'd known for a long time. God had always known. Perry was the one her heavenly

Father had chosen for her to love and cherish for a lifetime. Together they would worship and praise the Author and Anchor of their lives.

Oh God, thank You! she prayed. He had blessed her with everything she ever wanted. She would have a lifetime, and more, to marvel at His redeeming love.

Ava

11

Jenny

ARE YOU WILLING?

Jenny could not sit still. She was practically bouncing back and forth between the living room couch and a nearby chair. Every few seconds, she ran to the front window to peek out.

"He'll be here, Jenny," called her mother from the kitchen. "Just be patient."

"I know, Mom," Jenny answered. But it was hard to be patient. She was too excited!

Jenny's parents had divorced years ago. Now the energetic ten-year-old saw her father only on weekends. Fred Wyatt picked up his daughter every Friday after school. They would go to the movies, or shopping at Wal-Mart, or just hang out and watch cartoons together at Fred's apartment.

Jenny loved it. She adored her father, and relished being "Daddy's little girl." She spoke to him on the phone every night before she went to bed, but actually being with him on weekends was the best.

For what seemed the hundredth time that afternoon,

Jenny bounded to the window. This time she saw a white Ford Mustang pulling into the driveway.

"He's here!" she yelled. "'Bye, Mom!"

Jenny grabbed her backpack and pillow by the door and raced outside. "Hi, Dad!" she called.

Fred wore a T-shirt and jeans. His wavy brown hair was uncombed. He had a somber expression when he got out of the car, but it changed when he saw Jenny. He smiled and gave her a hug.

"I've got something for you," he whispered. He reached into his back pocket and pulled out a small package.

"Lion King cards!" Jenny said. She hugged her father again. "Can I open them now?"

"You bet," Fred said.

As they drove off, Jenny ripped apart the wrapper and described each card in detail to her father. Fred nodded as she spoke, but Jenny noticed he seemed distracted. He'd been so sad lately. She wanted to help him, but didn't know what to say.

Oh, well, she thought. *We're together again, and that's all that matters.*

~

It was a night about three years later that Jenny's world changed forever. She was babysitting at a neighbor's house. After tucking her charges into bed, she made her usual evening phone call to her dad. She was surprised when another man answered.

"Uh, hello," she said. "I'd like to talk to Fred, please."

There was a pause on the other end of the line. "He…I'm sorry, he can't come to the phone right now."

Jenny felt her skin prick. Something in the man's tone didn't sound right. "This is his daughter," she said. "Tell him I need to talk to him right now."

Jenny heard other voices in the background. "I'm sorry," the man said again. "He's not available. That's all I can say. I have to go now."

"Wait!" Jenny said. "What do you mean—?"

The phone went dead.

Jenny called her mom, Eva, who promised to check out what was going on. When the neighbor returned, Jenny hurried home. Kevin, her stepfather, asked Jenny and her mother to come into the living room and sit down.

Kevin waited until both were seated. Without further warning, he uttered the simple phrase Jenny would never forget: "Fred's dead."

"What?" Jenny said, her voice nearly a whisper.

Kevin looked down. "He killed himself today."

NO! Jenny thought. *Not Dad! No, no, no!*

She slid out of her chair, onto her knees, and stared at the beige carpet. She expected to cry, but nothing came out. The shock was too great.

This can't be happening, she thought. *It just can't.*

The days that followed were a blur for Jenny. She learned of a note from her dad that described her as his "constant joy." She attended his funeral. She had dreams of her dad calling her again on the phone, saying he'd only gone away and he'd be back in a little while. She was overwhelmed by feelings of shock, grief, and guilt. She felt as if she'd let her dad down, that somehow she should have been able to save him.

It was almost more than a thirteen-year-old could handle. Somewhere in the midst of those dark days, Jenny shut down her emotions. Feelings betrayed her, bringing only a tortured agony.

She decided she didn't want to feel anymore. Over the next two years, Jenny became quiet and withdrawn. She rarely smiled. It was almost as if she were sleepwalking.

Then, as a ninth grader starting high school, she discovered that drugs, drinking, and sex granted her a temporary escape from her misery. Yet it all caused more harm than good. Jenny grew insecure and even more detached, believing she didn't fit in with other students. During her sophomore year, she left the high school to begin a home-school program.

Jenny found a sliver of hope the following year. As a child she'd attended church occasionally and believed in God, but after the death of her father she found herself hating Him. She wanted nothing to do with a God who would allow something so awful in her life. In high school, however, when a friend invited her to a church retreat at the coast, she wavered.

It's probably better than sitting at home all weekend, Jenny thought. *Why not?*

The retreat featured Christian musicians performing under circus tents on the beach. At one point during an evening performance, Jenny found herself focusing intently on the words. They described a God who fills the need of every soul, who cares deeply about each of His children.

Something in that moment forged a crack in the stone wall Jenny had erected around her heart. She sat down and began to cry. She knew it was true—she *did* need God, despite the anger she'd felt before. She couldn't keep going on her own. She gave her life to the Lord right then. Immediately, she felt a difference.

For the next year, Jenny stayed away from drugs and tried to focus more on her relationship with God. Yet her insecurities were still so strong. She began dating a guy who hung around with the wrong crowd. Before she knew it, she was racing down a path that led to darkness. She took up drugs again. She dropped her studies and moved out of her mom's home. She took a job as a cocktail waitress and became addicted to crystal methamphetamine.

Jenny had put God "on hold."

One night after work, Jenny visited her boyfriend's house. She went into the bathroom to snort a line of meth, but stopped when she looked in the mirror. She barely recognized the person staring back at her. Her body was emaciated; she had a pale face, blue lips, and stringy brown hair. She looked dead.

Jenny couldn't believe that person was her. Stunned, she sat on the toilet lid.

How did things get this bad? she thought. *If I don't stop this, I'm going to die. God, I need help. If You can just get me through this night, I promise I'll stop doing drugs.*

When Jenny looked in the mirror a few moments later, she was amazed. She saw color in her cheeks and a spark in her eyes. She felt more alive. *Thanks, God!* she prayed.

The meth, however, was still in her pocket. For Jenny, drugs were the answer for every emotion—even joy. She was afraid to feel.

Within a few minutes, Jenny was high again, her promise forgotten. God was back on hold.

A few months later, Jenny was driving three friends to North Carolina. They'd been on the road in a torrential downpour for hours, and each had been snorting meth. Jenny felt paranoid. She imagined that her friends might attack her. She even turned off the radio, fearing that people were listening to their conversation through the airwaves.

Then a more ominous thought invaded Jenny's mind. It was suddenly clear to her that they were going to be in an accident.

They were passing through a small town in South Carolina when their headlights illuminated a small church on the side of the road. Jenny pulled into the puddle-filled parking lot.

"If we keep going, we're going to get in a wreck," she said. "I'm not driving another mile."

"Jenny, what are you talking about?" Sidney, her boyfriend, asked. "We're fine." The others agreed. Finally Sidney decided to drive. Jenny didn't want to be stranded, so she reluctantly agreed.

The car sped faster and faster as they moved out of the town and back onto the highway. Jenny could see a sharp turn in the road ahead, but the car wasn't slowing. Suddenly, she heard a woman's voice screaming—her own.

"Sidney, slow down!" she yelled. It was too late. The car missed the curve, crashed through a stand of trees, and headed toward an embankment on the far side of a creek. They hit.

Then there was nothing.

～

Jenny and the others survived the accident, but Jenny suffered a broken back and a badly damaged wrist. She underwent multiple surgeries and was placed in a body cast for three months.

The trauma of the accident and recovery sent Jenny into a new tailspin of depression and bad decisions. She went to live with her mother after being released from the hospital, and felt humiliated that Eva had to bathe her. She spent her car insurance settlement on drugs. She slept with Sidney's best friend and ended up making enemies of them both.

When Eva kicked Jenny out of the house for having drugs around her younger half-siblings, Jenny moved in with a friend. But the downward spiral continued. She experimented with new, even more dangerous drugs. She was taken to the hospital three times for accidental overdoses.

Finally, alone in her bedroom one night, Jenny cowered under the covers. She thought people were trying to kill her. She took a handful of pills, and then more pills as her paranoia increased.

"I'm going crazy," she said to herself. "I've completely lost it. I don't know what to do."

Jenny peered out of her bedroom and saw no one. She

checked behind the living room furniture to make sure she was alone, then walked toward the kitchen. There was a brochure lying on the dining room table.

Jenny picked the paper up. The brochure was called "Life After Death." She'd never seen it before. She couldn't imagine how it got there.

She began reading. Almost immediately, the words pierced her heart. It was as if God had dropped the brochure through the ceiling and said to Jenny, "You've put Me off long enough. I'm taking Myself off hold now."

Jenny went into her bedroom and fell to her knees. *Okay, God, I need help,* she prayed. *You're the only one who can help me here. I need a miracle.*

She put a finger down her throat and forced herself to vomit the pills. The days that followed were a constant battle between wanting to do more drugs and wanting to stop. She would snort a line of meth, then in disgust flush the rest down the toilet. But after a while, the craving would return, and she'd go out to buy more drugs.

One especially discouraging day, the desire for drugs again overwhelmed Jenny. In a panic, she ran upstairs to a friend's apartment where she'd partied before. When he answered the door, she said, "Phil, I really need some pills. What do you have?"

"You've come to the right place," Phil told her. He invited her in and led her to his bedroom. There he opened the door to a large wooden cabinet. Inside were several hundred bottles of almost every pill imaginable, each organized into sections by type. Some were for heart problems. Others were for nerves, headaches, or sleeplessness.

The sight scared Jenny. She could almost hear the Lord speaking to her: *Jenny, this is what you've been doing. Every time you begin to feel anything at all, you try to find something to take the feeling away.*

Oh, God, You are so right, Jenny prayed. *I don't like to feel.*

She told Phil she'd changed her mind and hurried back downstairs.

Jenny was twenty-one years old, and at a crossroads. During the following week, three people told Jenny that if she didn't stop doing drugs, she'd be dead before the age of twenty-two. She knew God was warning her. She had to do something—now.

Eva had done research on a pair of programs she thought might help her daughter, one of which was Wellspring. Jenny agreed to give Wellspring a try.

All of the girls who come to Wellspring are required to take a blood test to show they are clean when they enter the program. Jenny failed hers on multiple counts.

"Jenny, I'm sorry," one of our program directors told her. "You'll have to go back home. If you really want to be here, come back for another test in three days."

The next time, Jenny passed the test and was accepted into Wellspring. But failing the test the first time was a sign that her days with us would not all be easy.

Jenny struggled with her attitude toward all of us, especially in the first few weeks. For example, there was the time she said she couldn't make it to a class because she'd decided to dye her hair.

But much more serious was the day we discovered that another girl in the program, Mickey, had been smuggling drugs into the home and supplying them to Jenny. The fault lay not just with Mickey and Jenny. We promise to provide a safe atmosphere for every girl at Wellspring. We had let them down.

Yet even in the midst of these troubles, Jenny persevered in pursuing a deeper relationship with the Lord. Just before moving into the home, Jenny's mother had told her daughter about her own favorite verse, Philippians 4:13: "I can do everything through him who gives me strength." Jenny opened her Bible to those words many times during her days at Wellspring.

Jenny experienced a breakthrough about a month after she arrived. It was evening, and she was lying in bed at the end of the day. She was discouraged. The classes and her time with God seemed only to expose her weaknesses. She felt selfish, weak, and inadequate.

What am I doing here, God? she prayed. *I can't do all this. I don't know how to change or be what You want me to be.*

As Jenny stewed, a sudden sensation of peace washed over her. Then, so clearly that it could have been an audible voice, she felt God speaking to her. "Jenny, there is only one thing I want you to get out of Wellspring," He seemed to say. "I want you to love. I know that You love Me. Now love others, and love yourself."

It was a reaffirmation of the second commandment given by Jesus. It was also exactly what Jenny needed to hear.

Jenny began to forgive herself for the mistakes she'd made in her life. She discovered she *could* love herself and the people around her. Yet she still had trouble trusting others, especially men. With his suicide, her father had broken her heart. She felt that others—even God—would surely abandon her one day too.

I was so proud of Jenny on the day she graduated from Wellspring. She had worked so hard and learned so much. She hardly seemed like the same person I'd met a year before. Yet I also knew she would face more struggles in the days ahead. The process of giving herself to the Lord wouldn't happen in a single moment. It was a choice that she, like all of us, would have to make day after day, week after week, year after year.

That's why I wasn't totally surprised when she appeared on my doorstep one night, upset and discouraged. She was having car trouble. She was suffering from back pain. Her new friends didn't understand what she was going through.

"Mary Frances, I can't make it," she said. "I don't know what to do."

I wasn't sure what to tell Jenny. I didn't have any answers. But I knew Who did.

"Why don't you go down to the basement," I said. "Just spend twenty minutes or so reading Scripture. Then I'll come down and we'll talk."

Jenny did as I asked. When I saw her several minutes later, the tension in her face was gone.

"You were right," she said. "I just needed to pray and hear God's Word. I feel so much more at peace now."

Later, I thought about how often that had been the perfect response when Jenny or one of the girls in the program was struggling. My attempts at comfort and guidance could never match the eternal wisdom of Scripture. David put it best in Psalm 19:7–9: "The law of the LORD is perfect, reviving the soul. The statutes of the LORD are trustworthy, making wise the simple. The precepts of the LORD are right, giving joy to the heart. The commands of the LORD are radiant, giving light to the eyes. The fear of the LORD is pure, enduring forever. The ordinances of the LORD are sure and altogether righteous."

Jenny was learning to depend on God's law, and I could see it making a difference. Yet He wanted even more. He was after her heart.

Jenny knew that God loved her. But she began to understand just how important she was to God on a day she was driving home from her job at a missions organization in Atlanta. Heavy black clouds had turned a steady drizzle into a downpour. The rain hammering against the car brought back frightening memories of the car accident in South Carolina.

Suddenly, Jenny felt overwhelmed by an irrational fear. She believed she was going to crash again. She gripped the steering wheel so hard her hands hurt. She wanted to pull over, but she was trapped in freeway traffic.

God, please make it stop! Jenny prayed. It was a desperate plea.

Jenny

To Jenny's shock, the rain ceased immediately. A burst of sunshine pushed away the clouds.

Jenny breathed a sigh of relief and wonder. God had just done something supernatural, just for her. For maybe the first time since her earthly father's death, she felt like a daughter who was loved by her Father. After all these years, she was "Daddy's little girl" again.

It was a wonderful feeling.

A few weeks later, on her lunch break, Jenny met with me to talk about coming to work at Wellspring as an intern. She felt the Lord leading her to a new challenge. But it turned out He had more in mind than a job change.

On her way back to work, Jenny glanced through her windshield at a group of puffy white clouds overhead. As she looked, she realized the clouds weren't arranged randomly— she could see a pattern. They had formed a huge, beautiful, plump heart, with a hand wrapped around it.

Jenny sucked in a breath and held it. *Am I really seeing that?* She checked the road, then looked up again. It was still there.

At that moment, Jenny felt God's presence in the car with her. He was asking a single question: "Are you willing to give Me your heart?"

Jenny began to cry. She suddenly realized that as much as she loved God and knew that He loved her, she'd been holding back. She hadn't trusted Him completely.

Now He wanted everything.

"Yes, God," she whispered. "I want to do that."

Jenny's journey toward a closer relationship with the Lord has affected more than her own heart. For instance, she traveled to Morocco for a month-long mission trip, where she lived with a Muslim family and taught poor children. She also spent at year with us at Wellspring teaching classes and encouraging the girls in the program. She seemed to gravitate toward the ones with the greatest difficulties. Hailey, for instance, disliked herself so much that she frequently cut her own arms and legs. Jenny helped Hailey recognize her value and see her inner and outer beauty.

Jenny's influence on Nikki was even more profound. Nikki moved in with Jenny's family as a foster child when both girls were sixteen. Nikki ran away and was heavily involved in drugs. When she came back, Jenny was gone, enrolled in Wellspring.

"I visited her in the recovery home," Nikki said, "and I saw her in a totally different light. She had changed so much that I actually didn't recognize her. I wanted to know what happened, because my life was going downhill fast…I wanted what Jenny had."

Jenny prayed for Nikki every day for six months, and advocated her entrance into the program as well. Nikki did eventually join us; today, she is a graduate just like Jenny, thankful that "my awesome God has transformed me."

Jenny still struggles at times with trusting the Lord, and with trusting others. She's also dealing with anger at her father for abandoning her, which she's kept inside for years. But she has come so far. I knew she was a changed woman when she told me recently that her boyfriend, also a believer, had proposed to her and she'd said yes. She was ready to share her heart and life with another man.

"It's a process," she says of her healing. "I won't be 'fixed' today or even ten years from now. That won't happen until I die. But I'm leaning on God and trusting Him more than ever. I'm so excited to see what the future will be."

I am too. And I believe Jenny's Father in heaven feels the same way.

12

FREE

William Shakespeare once wrote, "Truth is truth to the end of reckoning." Yet to a child growing up within a murky fog of betrayal and deceit, truth can be as elusive as a lighthouse with a burned-out beacon.

Almost from the day she was born in a tiny town in Mississippi, Sarah received a confusing series of messages. Her father, Richard, treated her well, but he was physically and verbally abusive toward her mother and half-sister. Sarah's mother, Beth, took the family to church and taught Sunday school, but nothing they talked about there ever seemed to apply at home.

Sarah adored Ellen, her half-sister. She was seven years older, beautiful, and popular. But Ellen took out her anger at her stepfather, Sarah's father, on her little sister. She told Sarah, "You're fat, ugly, and stupid. You shouldn't even talk. Every time you open your mouth, you sound like an idiot."

Every word was a lie, but Sarah was too young to know it.

The worst betrayal of all began one winter evening when Sarah was five. Her parents were out of the house. Sarah pulled on worn pajamas, the ones with a picture of Daisy Duck on the front, and brushed her teeth. Ellen guided her to her bed. Sarah crawled in and cuddled up with her favorite stuffed bunny.

To Sarah's surprise, Ellen closed the door and turned off the light. Sarah always liked to have some light coming in. She was afraid of the dark.

"Ellen, why did you close the door?" she said.

Ellen didn't answer. Instead, she crossed the room and crawled into bed with Sarah. Then, to Sarah's shock, she began touching her in places Sarah knew she wasn't supposed to touch.

"Ellen," Sarah whimpered.

"Shut up," her older sister said.

Later, Ellen made Sarah promise not to say a word about what had happened. "If you tell," Ellen said, "I'll say that Richard did it, and they'll arrest him and take him away." It scared Sarah. She kept her mouth shut.

The sexual abuse continued for the next four years.

As it turned out, everyone in Sarah's family had secrets, which they covered with half-truths and outright lies. The secrets caught up with Sarah's family when she was nine. Richard discovered that Beth was having an affair; a divorce soon followed. The girls continued to live with their mother.

Sarah watched it all—and learned. If no one else told the truth in her family, she reasoned, then she wouldn't either.

Sarah

She survived by pretending that everything was all right. She was a sweet child, always doing what was expected of her and earning top marks at school. No one knew about the pain she felt inside.

After the divorce, Sarah missed her dad. Everything felt different at home—except for the lies.

For example, Sarah could tell when Beth was talking to another man on the phone. "Who was that, Mom?" she asked once after her mother hung up.

"Oh, just a girlfriend from work," Beth said. The deception made Sarah furious.

With her father gone, Sarah's sweet exterior was soon replaced with an angry one. She began hanging out with a new set of friends, a wild group that smoked and drank.

Beth remarried when Sarah was eleven, which brought a stepfather and stepbrother into their home. Ellen had stopped abusing Sarah, but now the much larger and stronger stepbrother began making advances toward her. Sarah fought him off, but she was terrified. She told her mother, but Beth couldn't or wouldn't do much about it.

Finally, after Sarah lived through three years of continual fear, her mother ended the marriage. The stepfather and stepbrother were gone.

After Ellen graduated from high school and also left home, Sarah found the courage to tell her mother about her sister's sexual abuse. But Beth hardly responded. She had a new man in her life, and she didn't want to upset him. Instead, she pretended as if the abuse never happened. It only reinforced what Sarah had already believed: To the people closest to her, the truth didn't much matter.

I don't know if she even believes me, Sarah thought. *Doesn't she know the truth when she hears it? Doesn't she even care?*

When she was sixteen, Sarah faced a new and frightening truth: She was pregnant. She wanted to marry her boyfriend and have the baby, but her mother was dead-set against the idea from the beginning. "If you have this baby," she told Sarah, "I'll never see you again." Sarah's only choice, Beth said, was to have an abortion.

Sarah resisted. She wanted to keep her baby. But she was terribly sick almost from the beginning of the pregnancy. She couldn't keep food down and lost twenty pounds in three weeks. Sarah's eyes turned dark red from bursting blood vessels, yet Beth refused to take her to the hospital. She was more concerned about her image in the eyes of her friends than her daughter's health. She didn't want anyone to know her daughter was pregnant.

Sarah could barely make it through each day. She couldn't see a way out. Meanwhile, Beth kept pressing for the abortion.

I don't want an abortion! Sarah's thoughts screamed. *But what else can I do? I feel like I'm dying.*

Sarah was twelve weeks along when she went to a clinic. The abortion was one more bad dream in what had become an ongoing nightmare.

When she graduated from high school, Sarah yearned for a chance to get away from Mississippi and start life fresh. Her boyfriend had joined the Marines after Beth refused to let him see Sarah. Now the promise of adventure and challenge in the services also beckoned to her. She thought about her grandfather, "Dr. Gil," who had always been so kind to her. He had his own family practice in Mississippi.

Maybe I could do that, Sarah thought. *I could be a medic and take care of people. Why not?*

She enlisted in the army.

Sarah proved to be a star soldier and was promoted quickly. She served as a medic for seven months in Bosnia as part of the NATO peacekeeping force, Operation Joint Forge.

Yet no matter where she was stationed, Sarah couldn't escape the feelings of bitterness and anger that had been building inside of her for years. Her work was rewarding, but sometimes she felt she was just going through the motions. Did any of it really matter?

And so she drank—often. She moved in and out of bad relationships. When she found out one boyfriend had cheated on her, she became so incensed that she attacked him. She started doing cocaine. Professionally, she had everything under control. Personally, she was a mess.

When her army term was up, Sarah reenlisted and was sent to Germany.

Okay, Sarah, she thought, *this is a new start. You're not going to do the same things again. You're not going to embarrass yourself by getting drunk all the time. You're not going to waste time on bad relationships. This time will be different.*

It wasn't. If anything, her drinking, drug abuse, and penchant for picking "Mr. Wrongs" grew worse.

The lowest moment, however, may have occurred back in Mississippi when Sarah was on leave. She was staying at her grandparents' home. That night, all three had plenty of wine with their dinner. Then Sarah said good nights and went to bed. When she woke up a couple of hours later, however, she discovered her grandfather there with his hands on her.

"Grandpa, what are you doing?" she cried, pushing him away.

He mumbled something incoherent.

He's drunk, she realized. She told Gil to go back to bed, and he did.

The incident rattled Sarah; she left the next morning. She didn't say anything about it to her grandmother. She knew it would break her heart.

It was one more betrayal, one more buried truth.

After three years of misery in Germany, Sarah was transferred to a teaching job at Fort Campbell, Kentucky, for the last year of her army commitment. There she met Jason, a six-foot-five Special Forces soldier with wavy black hair. Jason was Sarah's hero. She'd finally found someone she could trust, someone she was sure would rescue her from her life of lies and betrayal. It wasn't long before they were engaged.

But Jason had his own issues. He was an addict, hooked on cocaine and other women. After they married and moved to Florida, Sarah discovered that Jason had cheated on her during the engagement. They argued; he became physically abusive, once sending Sarah to the hospital with a separated rib.

On a morning that fall, sunlight stabbed through the blinds in Sarah's bedroom, creating strange shadows. They looked like spears trying to pierce her home. She thought they might pierce her heart as well.

Lying there alone, Sarah realized she wasn't safe with Jason. She needed to get away. Yet she was so depressed she didn't see the point. Why keep trying? Everyone lied to her. Everyone let her down. She couldn't depend on anyone else, and she couldn't hold things together by herself.

Sarah turned to God only in her darkest moments, and this was one of them.

"I can't do this anymore!" she screamed at the walls. "God, if You're there, help me!"

Something about that primal prayer calmed Sarah. She wasn't even sure why she was speaking to a God she didn't know, but in that moment, for the first time, she felt certain that He did exist.

Sarah found the will to leave Jason. She moved back to Mississippi, first living with her mother and then in her own apartment. She enrolled at the University of Mississippi. She seemed to have a new strength—cocaine no longer interested her, and for a time she stopped drinking as well. Only later would she believe that it was the Spirit of God beginning to work in her.

But Sarah was still a long way from being ready to give her heart to God. She gradually returned to alcohol. At first she had just a drink or two when she was out on the town, but she quickly progressed to regular binges.

Several concerned friends, both old and new, told Sarah that she needed help. One of them was Doug, an old crush from high school who played in a local Christian rock band. They'd kept in touch over the years. Doug seemed different than all the other men Sarah had dated, including Jason. He seemed honest, genuine. She'd been hurt so many times before that she wanted to hold back, yet she couldn't help herself—she fell in love.

When Doug also talked to Sarah about finding help for her drinking problem, she listened. But she wasn't willing to quit school and go to a clinic. She planned to deal with it later.

The last beam in the foundation of Sarah's resistance gave way on a muggy weekend in the spring. Sarah had taken her grandmother to a funeral, and she accepted her offer to stay at her house for dinner. Gil had made more strange advances in the months since that first night, but Sarah had still kept quiet about them in order to protect her grandmother. She was uncomfortable now, but figured she could handle a dinner with her grandparents.

Sarah refused any wine at first, but she relented when her grandmother insisted. Then Gil went to the kitchen to refill everyone's glasses. Sarah got through part of the second glass—and doesn't recall a single detail from the next day and a half. Today, she suspects that Gil slipped a drug into her drink. But whatever he might have had in mind for that night did not go as planned.

Sarah fell out of her chair at the dinner table. Even in her drugged state, she was putting things together. When she got back to her seat, she was belligerent and angry at her grandfather. She argued with Gil, and ended up telling her grandmother about Gil's inappropriate behavior. Sarah threatened Gil. Her grandmother called the police. Then Sarah passed out.

Sarah

A police officer was able to transport Sarah to her apartment parking lot without incident. But when he reached over her to unhook her seatbelt, Sarah went berserk. She repeatedly punched the surprised officer in the face. It eventually took three officers to wrestle a kicking and screaming Sarah—she was later described as "possessed"—back into a patrol car for a trip to the county jail.

After being released the next day, Sarah realized she needed help. She knew she had a drinking problem. But there was more than that going on inside her. Her anger, though often justified, was out of control.

I'm so tired of living like this, she thought. *I'm so sick of covering things up. I want the truth to come out—every last, ugly detail.*

Only two days before, someone had told Sarah's mother, Beth, about Wellspring. Beth had listened closely. She'd recently discovered and given her heart to Jesus. It changed everything for her. This time, she was ready to help her daughter.

Sarah, Beth, and Beth's new husband—also a believer—talked about Wellspring and another program they'd heard about. Sarah was leaning toward the other program, which asked for only a ten-week commitment instead of the twelve months we require at Wellspring. But she also felt a tugging toward our ministry.

They all decided to sleep on it. But as Sarah got ready for bed, someone knocked at her apartment door. It was the police. One of the officers had decided to file assault charges. Sarah was to be arrested and returned to jail immediately.

That night in her jail cell, Sarah prayed like she'd never prayed before. *God, I don't know what to do. I can't pretend I've got it under control anymore. Look at me—I'm in jail. Whatever You want, wherever You think I should go, it's in Your hands. Please show me what I should do.*

The next morning, Sarah and her attorney went before a judge and explained about the two programs they thought would help her. What they didn't know is that Sarah's new stepfather had called me early that morning at my home. I wasn't even supposed to be there, but I'd gone back into the house to retrieve my laptop. Could I, he asked, send a fax on Wellspring stationary right away to the judge and explain that we would accept Sarah?

A few minutes later, the judge received the fax. When he listened to Sarah and her uncle later that morning, he made the decision for them. "I think Wellspring is where you need to be," he said. "I'm going to release you on the condition that you enter the Wellspring program immediately."

Sarah couldn't wait. She was finally doing something positive to change the course of her life.

At Wellspring, Sarah was surprised to find that she adored the rest of the girls in the home. She'd never gotten along well with other women—probably because of her anger at her sister and mother—but in so many ways, these girls were just like her, hurting and trying to find a better way to live.

There was one exception: They all kept talking about Jesus.

I love their sweet hearts, Sarah thought, *but I think they're all a little nutty.*

Sarah believed in God at some level, but Christ was another matter. The idea of God sending His Son to live among men, die for them, and then be raised from the dead didn't connect with her. It all seemed too far-fetched, too miraculous.

Two weeks into the program, Sarah asked for a meeting with Aubrie, our program director.

"The program here at Wellspring is great," she said. "I can see how it's helping the other girls here. But it's all based on Christ, and I don't think I even believe in Jesus, so I don't see how I'm going to get healed here. I need *real* counseling."

Aubrie encouraged Sarah to give the program more time.

Sarah sighed. "I haven't decided for sure," she said. "But I just want to warn you that I'm pretty sure I need to start looking for another place."

After the meeting, Sarah wandered around the Wellspring Home, lost in thought. Where else would she go? Was leaving the right decision? But how could she be healed—how could even God heal her—if her heart wasn't in it?

She found herself downstairs in front of the open door to what we call the prayer closet. The tiny room, truly no larger than a utility closet, contained one chair upholstered in red and blue, a pillow on the floor, and a picture of Jesus and an angel on the wall.

Sarah stepped in, shut the door, and fell to her knees.

God, I'm so scared, she prayed. *I've made so many bad decisions. I just need to know what to do. Maybe I'm wrong about Wellspring. I trust You. Please tell me if I should go.*

A strange sensation came over Sarah. She felt a tugging in

her heart, and she somehow knew it was toward Wellspring. *But God,* she prayed, tears welling up in her eyes, *I don't even believe in Jesus. This is not going to work.*

The sensation grew stronger. It wasn't an audible voice, but Sarah nevertheless "heard" a response: *You need to stay. You're right where you need to be.*

Instantly a sense of calm washed over Sarah. She didn't understand or feel comfortable with everything she was hearing at Wellspring, but for the first time in her life, God had spoken to her. She was going to be all right.

Sarah was now at peace with her decision to stay at Wellspring, but not with her feelings about Christ. The more the other girls talked about Jesus, the more it drove Sarah crazy. She'd been deceived so many times in her life, had heard and seen so many lies. Yet what she believed about her faith, she realized, was the most important thing of all. What was the real truth?

Sarah began a quest for information. She read books. She asked questions. She searched her heart. She wanted to believe that Jesus Christ was the Son of God, but the facts and her feelings had to line up.

On the Thursday before Easter, Marsha, one of our volunteers, gave Sarah a book titled *The Case for Easter.* She read every word that day. For the first time in her life, it all made sense.

Sarah's heart was opening up. She knew she had to talk to God.

That evening she returned to the prayer closet. Once again she dropped to her knees, closed her eyes, and poured out her feelings to the Lord.

God, I desperately want to believe in Christ, she prayed. *The facts are there. I see what a difference He makes in people's lives. Yet something is holding me back. Please give me a way to believe.*

A few moments later, Sarah felt the Lord reminding her of the book of John and its description of the life and acts of Jesus. It was like unlocking a treasure chest in Sarah's heart. Everything Jesus had done, she had tried to do during her life—and had failed, because she'd relied only on herself. *God created us and loved us,* she thought. *He knew we'd never figure it out on our own, so He sent Jesus to die on the cross for us. But even more than that, He sent Jesus to show us how to* live.

It was the last step. Sarah could see it—and she believed.

With tears streaming down her face, she thanked God for answering her prayer, the most important prayer of all. "Dear God—dear Jesus," she whispered, "I ask You right now to be my Lord and Savior."

Some people experience God's grace gradually, like a gentle shower. For Sarah, the change was like tumbling down a roaring waterfall. She felt like a new person. Over the following days, Sarah discovered a spirit of forgiveness toward her sister, her mother, her grandfather, and so many others who had injured and abused her. She began to let go of the bitterness that controlled her and fueled her anger.

The changes in Sarah were obvious. Several weeks later, one of the new girls at Wellspring, Elyse, quietly approached her.

"Sarah, I can't believe you were ever an alcoholic," she said. "I've been watching you read your Bible. You talk about all this stuff like it's real. But sometimes, or maybe a lot of the time, I just don't get it."

Sarah's heart melted. Elyse was a mirror image of the person Sarah had been such a short time before—bitter, hurt, struggling with forgiveness, and searching for truth. "Forgiveness is the most freeing thing there is," Sarah told her. "Knowing I have forgiveness in Christ has saved me. I've been able to forgive the people who hurt me, but even better, I've been able to forgive myself. That's freedom."

As Sarah relayed her story to Elyse that evening and over the following weeks, Elyse began to open up and talk about the secrets of her own past. Sarah's encouragement has helped Elyse move a long way toward God and her own life of truth and freedom.

One freedom Sarah is giving up happily is the single life. She is engaged to marry Doug, her old crush from Mississippi. She is also contemplating a career helping others who struggle with drug and alcohol problems.

Sarah is reading Scripture and growing closer to Christ every day. John's Gospel, which has come to mean so much to her, includes this statement by Jesus: "If you hold to my teaching, you are really my disciples. Then you will know the truth, and the truth will set you free" (John 8:31–32).

Today, Sarah understands the meaning of those words. After a lifetime of feeling trapped by lies, she is free.

13

HOME

To little Boudhsalinh, not even three years old, the Maè Nam Khong—the "mother of all rivers"—was a wonder unlike anything she had ever before seen or heard.

Bundled in a tattered woolen coat and her warmest cap, Boudhsalinh stood on the deserted riverbank and watched, fascinated, as the river slid by in the moonlight. In the distance, she could hear the roar of falling water.

To the rest of her family, however, the river was not a wonder. It was the final obstacle in their desperate bid to escape. The family—Boudhsalinh's father, mother, and older brother and sister—had traveled all day, first by bus and then on foot, to reach this point many miles southeast of their modest home in Vientiane, Laos. They carried only a few possessions. Everything else was left behind so as not to arouse the suspicion of the communist government policemen who patrolled the streets and countryside.

Weeks ago, Boudhsalinh's mother, Buonyong, had found a job as a secretary at the American Embassy. The pay was better than anything she or her husband had earned before. But what seemed a blessing quickly became a curse. Strange men began to harass Buonyong on her way to and from the embassy and, more recently, when she was shopping for food. They accused her of treason for aiding the United States.

Then, two days ago, one man said he would kill her. Buonyong did not think it was an idle threat. Others thought to have ties to the Americans had disappeared recently. She and her family were no longer safe in their homeland. They had to flee.

On the riverbank that night, Buonyong gathered her children into a huddle around Boudhsalinh. She spoke softly and calmly to her offspring, but her eyes never stopped moving and scanning the area around them. Yanyong, Boudhsalinh's father, stood nearby, talking with a man dressed in dark clothing. Yanyong handed the man some money, then the stranger left.

"The boat is over there," Yanyong whispered to his family, pointing to a cluster of trees several meters away. Yanyong gathered Boudhsalinh in his arms and led the family toward the trees.

Boudhsalinh began to giggle loudly.

"No, Boudhsalinh!" Yanyong whispered in a cross voice. Boudhsalinh whimpered, then was silent. She didn't understand why her father's face was so angry and afraid. She couldn't know that he had recently heard about another family fleeing Laos by crossing the river into Thailand. That family had made it—except for their youngest, a boy barely six months old. His body had been found on the trail leading to the beach. The boy had been suffocated. Yanyong understood the terrible dilemma that family, probably the father, had faced. Guards were everywhere along the Maè Nam Khong, listening for the slightest sound, waiting for any excuse to imprison, torture, or kill runaways. The father's choice had been to either silence his beloved son and lose him, or lose everyone he loved.

It was not a choice Yanyong wanted to make.

The trees revealed a tiny, battered rowboat with only one oar and what appeared to be a hastily repaired hole in the bottom. A small bucket sat next to the hole. Yanyong cursed when he saw it.

"Will it keep us all afloat?" Buonyong whispered.

"It must," Yanyong said.

Boudhsalinh and her older brother and sister were placed in the rowboat, heads down on the wooden floor. Her sister cried out when her brother accidentally stepped on her hand, but she was silent after an angry glance from their father.

With Yanyong steering with the single oar and Buonyong holding Boudhsalinh in her arms, they pushed off. When water began seeping into the boat through the hole, Yanyong instructed his son to bail with the bucket.

A biting wind blew into Boudhsalinh's face. She saw they were surrounded by rushing water. The looming waterfall roared louder in her ears. She no longer felt the river was a wonder. Now she was afraid. She wanted to go home. She began to cry.

Buonyong tried to keep her daughter quiet, but Boudhsalinh was too upset. Suddenly, Boudhsalinh felt hands snatching her out of her mother's arms. It was her father. He clamped his hand over her mouth and held it there. She could breathe only through her nose.

"You must be quiet!" her father hissed.

Boudhsalinh stopped crying, but her father did not remove his hand until they were across the river and standing on the riverbank in Thailand.

Boudhsalinh whimpered again. She was tired, cold, and scared. She wanted to be home. But she would not feel at home for a very long time.

~

Boudhsalinh and her family lived in a refugee camp in Thailand for seven months. Then sponsors working with the Thai government arranged to transport them to America. They settled in Riverside, Georgia, a suburb of Atlanta.

To Boudhsalinh and the rest of her family, the American South was like another planet. No one in her family spoke English. Except for Buonyong's brief experience working at the U.S. embassy, none of them had ever been exposed to Americans or American culture. The familiar sights of rice fields and Buddha statues had been replaced by suburbs and strip malls. They were in a new world.

Boudhsalinh's parents began calling her "Carrie" in hopes it would help her fit into American society. The adjustment remained difficult, however. Carrie had trouble picking up the language. She had few friends at school. She was good at memorizing lessons in the classroom, but rarely understood what she was repeating.

Those problems were trifling, however, compared to the trauma that occurred when Carrie was eight years old.

One evening, Yanyong and Buonyong left their three children at their apartment for several hours with four of Yanyong's friends. The men scared Carrie. They'd been drinking, and began talking louder and laughing. One kept glancing in her direction.

Before Carrie realized what was happening, the man who'd been watching her came over, grabbed her hand, and took her into a bedroom. He took his clothes off, and insisted she do the same. Then he made her kiss him and began touching her.

Carrie knew that what the man was doing was wrong. She cried and told him to stop, but it made no difference. Later, she learned the same thing had happened to her sister and brother.

When Carrie told her parents about the incident, they didn't believe her. She was devastated, both by what had happened and that her parents believed she would lie about such things. She felt abandoned, worthless, and alone. She was a stranger in her own home.

Carrie got by during the next few years, at home and at school, but the negative feelings from that day never left her. In high school, desperate for a way to fit in, she began hanging out with a rebellious group of teens. She no longer saw the point in being a "good girl." Why not have a little fun? Drinking, drugs, and sex soon became a regular part of her life.

Then Carrie met Manny, a twenty-two-year-old with a dragon tattoo on his arm, when she got involved in a wild scheme to trick banks into cutting improper checks. The scheme didn't work—both were arrested—but Manny became infatuated with Carrie. She was flattered that some-one would take such interest in her. When Manny proposed marriage, she said yes. She was seventeen.

The marriage was rocky from the beginning. Carrie discovered her new husband was manipulative and verbally abusive. Yet she tried to make it work.

Three years into the marriage, Carrie learned she was pregnant. Her daughter Mali was born when she was twenty-one. A second daughter, Mya, arrived just eleven months later. Carrie loved her girls, but the responsibilities of parent-hood added new strains to her marriage. Not long after Mya's birth, Manny left Carrie, taking the girls with him.

Carrie fell into depression. Her drinking increased. She smoked marijuana often. She wanted her daughters back, but Manny refused. Finally, with the help of a friend, Carrie "kid-napped" Mali. Manny was furious, but a few months later, overwhelmed by the demands of single parenting, he relented and returned Mya to Carrie also.

Though she was overjoyed to have her daughters again, Carrie faced a new problem. She had few skills, and had barely been able to support herself when she was alone. Now she had two children to feed as well. What was she going to do?

A friend offered a solution. She was a dancer at an Atlanta strip club and made good money. Over lunch in Carrie's apartment, she said Carrie's natural beauty and exotic appearance would make her an instant hit in the clubs—and solve all her financial worries. "Once you get used to it, it's not as weird as it sounds," the friend said. "Just try it. What have you got to lose?"

"No way," Carrie said. "I'm not taking my clothes off in public. I couldn't handle it."

But that night, with Mali and Mya both hungry and crying and her refrigerator nearly empty, Carrie began to reconsider. *I have to make more money,* she thought. *How else are we going to survive?*

A few weeks later, Carrie debuted as a dancer at The Golden Canary. It took several beers beforehand for her to get up the nerve to go onstage. It was frightening to think about how everyone would be watching her. Yet somehow, she made it through.

Carrie danced again a few days later. The money *was* good, as her friend had promised. But she never felt comfortable on stage, and never got used to the prying eyes of the men in the crowd. It took more and more drinks, and then harder and harder drugs, for her to get through each performance.

Carrie danced in clubs for the next five years. By doing so she was able to support her family, but the cost of that support was enormous. She suffered panic attacks and often had thoughts of suicide. She mixed her anti-depression medication with Ecstasy, the synthetic depressant GHB, and other hard drugs. Several overdoses led to emergency visits from paramedics and ambulance trips to the hospital.

On the day Carrie visited a doctor's office to get a new prescription for anti-depression pills, she was nearly ready to give up. She felt like there was nothing to live for. She had no close friends. Her family was distant and didn't understand her. Her daughters, she felt, would be better off without her.

As Carrie sat alone in a waiting room, a nurse she'd seen before approached.

"You're Carrie, aren't you?" the nurse said.

Carrie nodded.

"Here," the nurse said, holding out a brochure. "You might take a look at that. I've heard good things about them."

Carried read the brochure. It described a ministry that offered hope and a way out for strip club dancers.

Can anyone really help me? Carrie wondered. *Is there any point in trying?*

Carrie wrestled with those questions for the next three days. Finally, she decided it was worth one last shot. She picked up a phone and called the ministry. As Carrie poured out her troubles and answered questions, she felt for the first time that someone was trying to understand her and her problems. She began hearing about a man who was God—Jesus Christ. She also heard about another ministry called Wellspring.

The more Carrie talked to her new friends at the ministry, the more she realized that she needed to learn more about this Jesus, and that she needed a place to do that. Her application to Wellspring was accepted soon thereafter. A church family volunteered to keep her kids during the six months

Carrie would live in the home. As the details fell into place, Carrie wondered if the man they called Jesus was working everything out.

Carrie started the program in November 2003. On the Wednesday before Thanksgiving, she spent the day with me and helped me prepare our house for guests coming the next day. She was a hard worker, and we had wonderful conversations that afternoon. There was something fragile and innocent about Carrie. Everything was new to her. Only the day before, she'd learned that we celebrate Christmas to honor Jesus' birthday.

"I just found that out!" she told me in an enthusiastic voice. "I never knew. But if Christmas is about God and Jesus," she said, her voice suddenly turning indignant, "then what is it with this Santa Claus? Why is there a Santa Claus? I don't understand that!"

I laughed. "That's a good question, Carrie," I said. "I don't know if I really understand that either."

About two weeks later, Carrie sat in the living room of the Wellspring Home and prepared to watch a movie about Jesus with Karen, a member of our staff. Karen had recently realized that Carrie was having trouble understanding the teaching in our classes. Her comprehension of written English was still underdeveloped, and her background in a Buddhist culture gave her no point of reference for even the most basic Christian doctrine. It was clear that Carrie wanted to understand but often just didn't get it. Karen had decided that in order to comprehend the message of the gospel, Carrie needed to "see" the story of Jesus.

As Karen pushed play to start the movie, she stifled a yawn. After all, she'd seen this story so many times. She knew every detail and plot twist.

Yet as Karen watched Carrie grow absorbed in the movie, sitting cross-legged on the floor and leaning close to hear every word, she realized that this young woman was experiencing the full power of the gospel for the first time. Through Carrie's eyes, Karen began to take in the story of Christ's life as if she too were watching it for the first time. Unexpectedly, Karen felt her heart being transformed too as she witnessed the images of God come to earth.

The movie played on. When Carrie watched Roman soldiers mock and torment Jesus, her contorted face revealed her inner distress. At this point, Karen stopped the movie.

"Why are they doing that to Jesus?" Carrie asked.

"Jesus is allowing that to happen for you and me," Karen said, feeling distressed herself. "He is paying the price for all of our sins, guilt, and shame. A sacrifice had to be made because the penalty of sin is death. Jesus is paying our penalty."

Karen resumed the movie. As Carrie watched Jesus' crucifixion and burial, tears rolled down her face. Then came the empty tomb and the proof of Jesus' resurrection. When Carrie saw the risen Jesus, she began to jump up and down on her knees in excitement. "He's alive!" she said.

From that moment on, Carrie was in love with Jesus. She was thrilled when the girls at the home made a birthday cake for Him as Christmas approached. But the highlight of the season was when she spent Christmas weekend with her daughters and the Parker family, who were caring for the girls. Mali and Mya had also been learning about Christ. They were ready to join their mother in committing their lives to Him.

On Christmas Eve, with candles adding a glow to the living room and Christmas music playing softly in the background, Carrie, her daughters, and the Parkers gathered to pray. Mali and Mya both knelt down in front of the sofa and closed their eyes.

"Dear Jesus," Mali prayed. "Please come into my heart."

In a tiny voice, Mya repeated the same prayer.

"And thank You, God, for Jesus' birthday," Mali added. "And for Christmas, and all the presents, and that Mommy found Jesus, and thank You for the Wellspring Home for saving my mommy."

Carrie's eyes welled up with tears as she listened to her children pray. *Thank You, Jesus,* she silently added. *This is the most wonderful moment of my life.*

Back in the home, Carrie devoured every class reading assignment and studied her Bible whenever she could. In fact, she carried it with her everywhere, even on trips to the grocery store. It became her lifeline.

Carrie also peppered everyone around her with questions. "What is faith?" "What is sin?" "What is guilt?" Her curiosity led the members of our staff into a better understanding of their own faith. As so often happens in the home, we learned as much as we taught.

Carrie was well-liked by the other girls in the program. Her enthusiasm rubbed off, and she often had an encouraging word for them. Because of her almost childlike appearance—she was barely five feet tall—and because she had so much trouble understanding American culture, the other girls found themselves forgetting about their own problems and jumping in to assist or explain things to Carrie. Everyone wanted to help her.

Besides, she could cook! All the girls took turns preparing meals, but Carrie's ability to create delectable Asian-themed feasts quickly made her Wellspring's most popular chef.

After weeks of Bible study and life lessons, we could see a difference in Carrie. She seemed more comfortable with herself. Her spiritual knowledge and maturity had expanded enormously. Day by day, she was starting to "get it."

The nights, however, were another story. It was almost as if the forces of darkness tried to make up for the ground they lost during the day with a coordinated attack at bedtime. Many times, a coach woke up to the sound of a tap on her door.

"I can't sleep," Carrie would say. "There's something in my room."

Carrie was plagued by visions of dark shapes flying above her and disturbing voices echoing in her mind. Too often, she would get up the next day exhausted after little or no sleep.

That began to change when Carrie moved in with the Conrads, her host family. By the time Carrie completed her six months in the Wellspring Home, she had made unbelievable strides. She possessed an entirely new and hope-filled concept of faith. She had her daughters back with her in the host home, and she slept in the same bedroom with them. That seemed to relieve most of the night visions.

And just as they had when Carrie was in the home, several people stepped up to help Carrie now that she was leaving. One family donated a jeep. Another helped her find a job at a computer retail store.

Despite these blessings, though, I knew that Carrie's faith was still fragile. Would she maintain her trust in and dependence on God? The test would come in the weeks ahead.

Alma Conrad, Carrie's host mom, soon noticed that Carrie had yet to develop many mothering skills. Mali, at just six years of age, was the organizer in their little family. Before the bus came for school, she made sure everyone had a lunch to take and was ready to leave. Alma had many long conversations with Carrie about the role and responsibilities of a mother.

Carrie also faced the challenge of learning a new job, budgeting, and all the other duties of "normal" life. For someone who had spent most of her adult years either drunk or high, it was a sometimes overwhelming change. Carrie frequently grew impatient and frustrated. She wasn't comfortable with this lifestyle. As was the case so often before, she didn't feel she belonged.

Carrie worked hard at being a better mother and at understanding what it took to be an office employee. She also continued her Bible study times. When she completed her three-month stay with the Conrads, she had new skills and an even stronger foundation in the Lord. She was a certified Wellspring graduate. But her biggest test was just beginning.

On her return to the "real world," Carrie struggled emotionally and spiritually. She tried to trust God, but sometimes wondered if He truly had the power to help her do things His way. When Laura, one of our coaches, called to check in on Carrie, the answer was usually, "Well, I'm breathin'. I'm still alive." Laura always did her best to encourage Carrie.

Finally, however, Carrie couldn't take it anymore. Everything was too hard and too new. She just wanted a place that was familiar, a place that felt like "home."

She went back to the strip clubs.

When Carrie walked into the door at The Golden Canary, her old boss, other employees, and old friends greeted her with smiles and hugs. It felt great to be remembered and welcomed. When they offered Carrie her old job back, she said yes.

She was a dancer again.

This time, however, Carrie couldn't bring herself to drink or do any drugs before going onstage. It just didn't feel right.

Dancing and stripping in front of an audience didn't feel right, either. It was familiar—the hot lights, the music, the haze of cigarette smoke, and of course the men watching every move—but it left her feeling uncomfortable and ashamed.

Back in the dressing room, Carrie buried her face in her hands.

Lord, You don't want me to be here, do You? she prayed. *I don't belong here anymore. Where am I supposed to go? Where do I belong?*

Even as she asked the question, Carrie realized she knew the answer. It had been in her heart for a long time. She just hadn't been willing to face it.

It doesn't matter where I go, does it Lord? she prayed. *It's not about a place at all. It's You. I belong to You now. My home is with You.*

Carrie left the clubs for good that night. She decided it was time to put her full trust in God.

At the Lord's leading, Carrie began to fill her schedule with new activities. She joined a weekly support group for former addicts to alcohol and drugs. She enrolled in a weekly parenting class based on biblical principles. She started helping with a ministry that reaches out to strip club dancers. She began encouraging other single mothers in a group at her church.

Recently, Laura again called to check in on Carrie. It had been a discouraging week for Laura. By the end of their conversation, it was Carrie who was helping lift Laura's spirits.

"You know, God is in control," Carrie told Laura. "You can trust Him. You can count on Him."

Today, Carrie is taking that advice.

"I feel like the pieces are coming together," Carrie told me when I stopped by recently for an afternoon visit at her apartment. We sat on her sofa and sipped tea together.

"I've learned that my way doesn't work," she continued. "Now I want to do everything God's way. I want to keep learning, be the best mom ever, and teach my children the truth so they can teach their children."

As Carrie talked about her daughters, I couldn't help but

notice the framed color photos of Mali and Mya on an end table, as well as their artwork displayed on the refrigerator. She was obviously proud of them, and I was proud of Carrie. She'd made a comfortable, loving home for her family, and I told her so.

"I'm just so thankful that God is with me, helping me and guiding me," Carrie said. "I know He loves me and that I belong to Him. He is my home. That's all that matters."

14

I SURRENDER

The young women who enter the Wellspring program have experienced some of the most horrible things I can imagine: emotional, physical, and sexual abuse; drug addition; prostitution; abortion. For most of their lives, they have known only confusion and pain. They join us looking for relief and guidance and quickly learn to lean on the wonderful live-in coaches—women about their same age, sometimes younger—who are so vital to everything we do.

The girls in the program look up to the coaches. I'm sure many of them, at least at first, believe that our coaches have always enjoyed intimate relationships with the Lord, have always understood His will, have always known the right thing to do—and done it. Of course, that isn't the case. The coaches in the home are learning and growing in Christ right along with the rest of the girls. Laura, our first coach, had no experience with the traumas that most of our participants have been through. She grew up in a Christian home, knew almost nothing about drugs, and had never even heard of "tricks" or "pimps."

She did, however, have a deep understanding of confusion and pain.

~

Laura stared at the doorknob. Behind it was the hallway of her apartment complex, and beyond that a city of half a million Chinese people. Laura was part of an organization that sent Christians overseas to teach English. She'd been in the country for eight months, and had made inroads with several of the students in her class. Some were showing a discreet interest in hearing more about Christ. Laura knew she should have been happy about the way things were going.

Instead, she was terrified.

The first six months had been a wonderful challenge. But as the excitement of living in a foreign country wore off and she settled into a routine, Laura battled increasing bouts of depression. She was lonely and fearful. The fear fed on itself, leading to panic attacks. She was afraid to watch TV, thinking it would trigger another attack. She would crawl into bed, curl into a ball, and ask God to comfort her as He had in years past. But now there was no response. She felt as though God had deserted her.

On this gray winter day, with her eyes fixed on the doorknob, Laura willed herself to overcome her anxiety. She needed groceries; she had to eat.

It's just a doorknob, Laura told herself. *You can do this.*

Finally, her trembling hand reached out and turned the knob. She moved deliberately through the dimly lit hallway, then down the first of five flights of steps. "You're going to be okay," she whispered.

She reached the bottom, stepped into a long alley, and blinked at the sudden daylight. It took all of her courage to keep going. The alley was filled with people riding bicycles and rummaging through dumpsters. Everyone was dressed in muted colors—long navy-blue jackets and gray button-up shirts.

Laura tried to ignore the crowd and walked ahead. She repeated verses from Philippians to help her concentrate.

A little farther down the alley, she came to a school playground full of children. Next to the basketball court she saw a bright red Communist flag hanging limply on a flagpole; it seemed out of place in the drab environment. The children stopped their games and ran to the fence to stare and wave at the foreigner. A flicker of a smile passed over Laura's face, but she knew she mustn't stop. She had to keep going.

"You're going to be okay," she repeated. Despite the cool weather, she could feel sweat on her forehead.

Finally the alley opened into a street lined on both sides with vendors in booths selling fruit, vegetables, ice cream, photo supplies, and more. The street itself was jammed with people going every direction. The store wasn't far now.

But as Laura pressed into the crowd, she was overwhelmed by the crush of people, sounds, and smells. She panicked. *No!* she thought. *I can't make it.*

Laura turned and began running. When she reached her

apartment, she threw herself onto her bed and cried.

This wasn't the life Laura had imagined growing up. She gave her heart to God as an eighth-grader in Peachtree City, Georgia. From that moment forward, she committed herself to being a nicer person and felt drawn to reading God's Word. In high school, she began to sense a call to ministry. She enrolled in Berry College, a Georgia liberal arts school with a Christian emphasis.

Laura was shy and felt insecure at Berry. But during her sophomore year, a senior named Melissa took an interest in her. She invited Laura to her apartment, where they enjoyed a meal of chicken and broccoli and talked about college, life, and God.

Melissa gave Laura a book called *Victory Over the Darkness*. "Laura, I want to invest in you," Melissa said. "I think this book would help you. If you are willing, I'd like to meet with you once a week and go through it with you."

Laura was floored. She couldn't believe this sophisticated senior cared about her and wanted to spend time with her. It was the beginning of a new attitude for Laura. She found herself focused less on herself and more on the needs of the people around her.

When Laura was a senior, she began reaching out to freshmen and sophomore girls on campus, just as Melissa had done for her. She volunteered with other ministries as well. She felt she'd found her calling.

This is so fulfilling, Lord, she prayed. *I want to do this for the rest of my life.*

One night while driving on campus, Laura received an

impression she felt was from God, telling her that she would be going on a mission trip to China. She was less than enthused; she hated flying.

God, You know how much I don't like to fly, she prayed. *If You really want me to go to China, then when I turn on my radio, they need to be talking about China.*

Laura flicked on the car radio. The announcer's first words were, "Today in Beijing…"

Still Laura put thoughts of China out of her mind. As much as she wanted to follow the will of God, she wasn't yet ready to surrender *everything*.

Laura graduated from Berry and spent the summer as a leader of a missions effort in Panama City Beach, Florida. It was rewarding work. She felt more drawn to the Lord than ever. One night when she was with her team on the beach, she walked to a secluded spot to pray and watch the stars. She sat down, took her sandals off, and let the still-warm sand run through her toes.

God spoke to her in that peaceful moment. It wasn't an audible voice, yet it was almost as clear as if He was sitting next to her. *Laura,* He seemed to say, *I want to use your life to reach generations.*

Laura recalled a verse that held deep meaning for her during her years at Berry, John 12:24. It contained the words of Jesus: "Unless a kernel of wheat falls to the ground and dies, it remains only a single seed. But if it dies, it produces many seeds."

She desperately wanted to be like that seed, to be a woman who dies to her own interests but is used to meet the needs of many. "Lord," she prayed, "whatever it takes to make that happen, please do it."

Laura had no idea then how much pain—and how much joy—would spring from that simple invitation.

During the next few years, Laura got involved in a singles group ministry at a church in Peachtree City. At the same time, an idea began to form. She dreamed about establishing a home for young women, a place where people could live, learn about God, and not have to worry about expenses. She grew discouraged, however, after sharing the idea with others. Everyone was polite, but most of the looks she received seemed to say, "Aren't you cute. But you know, no one's going to do that. Maybe you should think about finding a real job."

Then the idea of a trip to China returned. Again, Laura resisted.

"God, I don't think this is from You," she said. "But I want to be in Your will. If it is You, You'll have to bring me an application to show me I should go."

Laura worked at her church as a secretary. The next day at work she ran into an elderly woman she knew, Flo, who had been involved in a number of missions trips.

"Oh, hello, Laura," Flo said. "I just left something for you on your desk that I thought you might be interested in."

When Laura returned to her office, she opened the envelope. Inside was an application form for a Christian program that sent English teachers to China.

Laura sat down and stared at the form in her hand. *Okay, God,* she prayed. *I think I'm starting to get the message.*

That summer, as a "practice run," Laura flew to Jamaica

for a short-term mission trip. To her surprise, the flights didn't bother her at all. Soon she was collecting funds for the trip to China. Despite the high cost—$12,000—she raised every penny she needed.

Before she knew it, Laura was on a plane bound for the Far East.

The eleven-month stay in China turned out to be both heartening and devastating. Laura was thrilled that several students came to know Christ through their encounters with her. But the emotional toll was almost unbearable. It was as if all the fears and insecurities she'd felt during her life had joined forces to attack in a single, concentrated assault. During her final weeks in the country, it took all of Laura's strength to hang on until she could come home. Only later would she understand that she was enduring a spiritual battle with the highest of stakes.

Laura was overjoyed and relieved to return to the United States. Yet just days later, on a Saturday night, the pain returned. It was twice as bad as anything she'd experienced before. She felt as if she were being tortured from the inside out.

Before she could banish it, this thought entered her mind: *Go downstairs, get a knife, and end it.* She knew it was the enemy's voice.

This is ridiculous, she told herself. *I don't want to kill myself. I want to live!*

The next morning, Laura went back to her church with a terrible knot in her stomach. She didn't feel up to seeing all her old friends, but she knew she needed help. After the service, she explained her situation to her pastor, Kenneth Brown, who put her in touch with a counselor.

During the days that followed, Laura received a message from the Lord telling her to rest for the next six months. In her mind Laura began to protest; after all, she had financial responsibilities. But then she thought better of it.

He is God, after all, she mused. *Maybe I'd better listen on this one.*

As it turned out, Laura received some unexpected funds during those six months. Her finances never became an issue.

Laura's battles with fear continued. Her counselor suggested she go on a vacation with her family. Reluctantly, she agreed. When Laura checked into an eleventh-floor condominium in Florida with her parents, she chose a back room, away from the balcony overlooking the beach. She was afraid that if she got too close, she might throw herself over the edge.

One night during that vacation, Laura sat alone in her room, writing in her journal and talking with God. *Lord, what are You doing with me here?* she prayed. *I can't seem to do anything. My life is falling apart.*

Once again, Laura felt a response from God, as clear as if it was an audible voice: "Laura, I want you to surrender your emotional state of being to Me."

Surrender my emotions? Laura thought. *Can I really do that? How?*

She thought some more, and decided to write out a "contract" in her journal. In bold letters she printed: "I, Laura Warner, do hereby give up the right to my emotional state to my Lord Jesus Christ." She drew a signature line underneath and prepared to sign.

Then she hesitated.

If I sign this contract, she thought, *He could do anything. He could send those people in white coats to take me away and put me in an asylum. Is that what I want?*

Laura shook her head. *I know God works for my good,* she thought. *Even if He puts me away, He knows what He's doing. It would be stupid not to sign.*

Laura took her pen and filled in her signature. As she did, she felt a sudden welcome release.

No, her problems and fears did not suddenly disappear. But after that evening Laura's panic attacks gradually lessened and a sense of peace grew. More and more, she was able to hand over her anxieties to the Lord. Signing the contract with God had been a turning point. Laura finally understood that the key to victory in this battle was to surrender.

A few weeks later, as Laura was lying in bed one morning, the Lord spoke to her yet again. *Laura, remember the dream you had about the home for women? That time is now.*

God, what do You mean, now? she thought. *I'm still too messed up. I can't do anything.* She asked a pastor about it, but he hadn't heard of any programs like that.

What Laura didn't know was that I was in the early stages of establishing Wellspring, and had been praying fervently about who would be the right person to join us as our first live-in coach. When I prayed, God gave me Laura's name.

When I saw Laura in the church hallway a few days later,

I didn't know anything about the difficulties she was going through. I just knew that God wanted me to ask.

After we exchanged greetings, I explained what we were doing. "Laura, I think you're supposed to be involved in this," I said. "Would you consider working with us?" The more I told her about Wellspring, the wider her eyes grew.

Laura committed to us just a few weeks later.

Danielle, a twenty-four-year-old victim of sexual abuse who had fallen into drug use and prostitution, was our first "Wellspring girl." Laura, just two years older, would be her mentor. At that time we didn't yet have a home, or even an established program. But we all felt called to love and serve; we believed that the details would come later.

Laura and Danielle moved into a rented condominium and began growing in God together. It wasn't always easy. In the first week alone, Danielle became upset because we weren't finding a home quickly enough for her dog, Libby.

"Y'all don't care about me or my dog!" she yelled at Laura.

The raw emotion was too much for Laura. She began to cry and retreated to her room. *Lord, what am I doing here?* she prayed through tears. *I don't know how to help this person.*

A few minutes later, Danielle crept in and knelt beside Laura. With tears in her eyes, Danielle told Laura, "I did not mean to hurt you. I know you all care for me. You've been wonderful to me." Then she left.

Soon, to Danielle's surprise, Laura returned the favor and checked in on Danielle. They talked about what had happened and worked through the conflict. It was an important moment for both of them. Laura learned that she could weather the tough times, and Danielle discovered that she would be forgiven for her mistakes.

Laura served as a live-in coach for the next three years, with God healing her at the same time He was healing the girls in the program. Laura often felt that in her walk with God, she was only half a day ahead of the girls she was mentoring.

One of Laura's hardest times in the home was a period where she kept hearing disturbing voices in her head. She wondered if she was going crazy. One afternoon shortly after the voices began, Joy, one of the Wellspring girls, pulled Laura aside.

"Laura," she asked quietly, "do you ever feel like you have voices inside your head?"

Both young women soon realized they weren't alone in their struggles.

A day or two later, while driving across town, Laura stifled a yawn. The incessant voices were keeping her from sleeping. She was exhausted.

I'm going to try praying, she thought. She closed her eyes at a stoplight and spoke out loud: "In the name of the Lord Jesus Christ, to any voice in my head that is not of Jesus Christ, you must be silent."

Instantly, the voices ceased.

"Are you kidding?" Laura said to herself in the sudden quiet. "Thank You, Lord. That's amazing!"

For Laura, it was a lesson in the authority of Christ. She understood more than ever before that spiritual battles are real, but that victory is always possible through God. It provided her with an added boost of encouragement, as well as a new tool to give the girls in the home.

Even more encouraging was the spiritual encounter she witnessed on another evening in the home. Laura was in bed when a tap sounded at her door. It was Connie and her roommate, Carrie.

"Laura, you've got to pray for Carrie," Connie said. "She can't sleep and neither can I."

Carrie, who had only joined us a few weeks ago, wasn't even sure what the problem was. "I can't explain it," she said. "Something's just wrong."

Laura and the other girls knelt on the floor and held hands. As they talked, Laura was shocked by a vision. Behind Carrie she could "see" a sea of men. There were thousands of indistinguishable faces.

"Carrie," Laura said in wonder, "have you ever asked Christ to come and break your ties with all the men you've been with?"

"What do you mean?" Carrie asked.

Laura explained how Jesus could break "soul ties" with anyone who had controlled Carrie either spiritually, emotionally, or physically.

"Yes," Carrie said. "I want to do that."

While still holding hands, Laura prayed for Christ's presence to fill the room and remove any unwanted connections between Carrie and men in her past. She paused, and Carrie picked up the prayer, also asking the Lord to intervene and sever her ties to these men.

"Lord, please take all the pieces of my heart that I have

given away and give them back to me. Make me whole again," Carrie said. "Thank You, Lord, for loving me. Thank You."

Carrie kept praying, her voice growing stronger and faster. She squeezed Laura's hand so hard it hurt.

After several minutes of fervent prayer, Carrie finished. Laura rubbed her hand and looked at her. "Carrie, you were so excited during that prayer," she said. "What was going on?"

Carrie laughed, her eyes dancing. "I've never felt that much love before," she said. "I felt like God was putting my heart back together. It was wonderful!"

For Laura, it was more evidence of the Lord's love and supernatural power. He was healing and freeing the broken women of Wellspring right before her eyes.

Thank You, Lord, she prayed. *It is such a privilege to be even a small part of this. You are truly an awesome God.*

The girls in the home feel privileged to have had Laura as a coach. Many have stayed in touch with her after they graduated. Danielle recently invited Laura to be in her wedding. Today, Laura is a Wellspring program director in charge of supporting the coaches and meeting with the staff to pray.

"When I started as a coach, I didn't feel I had that much in common with the girls," Laura says. "I was very much in the minority. But we all have the same basic needs—to know that we matter, to know that we are loved and cared for. We all choose different ways to meet those needs, and some are more socially acceptable than others. Yet the main thing isn't figuring out what's socially acceptable. It's letting Christ fill our needs."

That can be hard to do for a young woman who has trusted in others, only to have that trust repeatedly broken. But as Laura has discovered, it makes all the difference.

"I've learned that we really can trust God," she says. "If we surrender everything to Him, He is enough."

IN CLOSING

For most of my life, I never thought of myself as a dangerous woman. I was a "good girl" while growing up in the small town of Geneva, Alabama. I married my high school sweetheart. I planned to become a mom and kindergarten teacher, to shape the lives of little children for twenty years, and then retire.

God had something else in mind.

As the younger sibling of a brother with Down's syndrome, I learned to be a protector and comforter early in life. Then, when my marriage ripped apart, I learned that a broken heart was more than a catchy phrase. I felt devastated—broken beyond repair.

That's where God came in. He'd always been part of my life, but now He became my lifeline. The more I sought Him, the greater my sense of healing and comfort.

As I fell in love with the Lord and His Word, I discovered a deep-seated desire—some might call it a dangerous passion—to help those who were hurting discover Him too. Through my church I found a group of like-minded people, and that is how our "league of dangerous women" was born.

After reading this book, you may be feeling a new or

greater urgency to reach out to lost, confused, and wounded souls. If so, I urge you to embrace it with all your heart! There is nothing quite like the fulfillment and joy that comes from answering God's call to be dangerous for Him.

In my journey at Wellspring, I've discovered that I'm most effective at touching the hearts of our girls when I learn to love them unconditionally. It's so easy to focus on their behaviors instead of what's going on inside, but I know they need compassion, not condemnation. I show that I care by trying to meet their basic needs. I'll ask if they've eaten, if they have money for gas, if I can pray for them. I try to encourage them through notes, conversations, and little gifts. By gently, consistently working to win their trust and waiting patiently upon God's timing, I've found that they usually overcome the wariness built up from years of betrayal. Eventually, they let me into their lives.

Perhaps the most important lesson I've learned, however, is that I can't save anyone from herself. As much as I want to help each girl I meet at Wellspring, I am not responsible for her healing.

Do you know the story of Jesus and the paralytic from the book of Mark? Four friends carried a paralyzed man on a mat to a home where Jesus was teaching. It was too crowded to go in through the door, so they made a hole in the roof and lowered the man to Jesus. The men could do nothing for their paralyzed friend, but they knew Jesus could. Moved by the faith of these men, Christ healed the paralytic.

In the same way, we cannot heal the brokenhearted on our own. We can only take them to the One who can. My prayer is that you will surrender your heart to the Lord, find the courage to step out of your comfortable lifestyle, and risk becoming dangerous by leading the lost to Him. A hurting world is waiting for you.

Finally, I realize that you may be in a very different place as you finish this book—you may be wounded and broken yourself. If so, I want you to know that you are valuable beyond measure, that somewhere nearby are people ready to help and care for you, and that the God of heaven and earth loves you more than you can imagine. My heart goes out to you as you struggle to get through each day. I don't have the solutions to all of the challenges you're facing, but there is One who does.

In Him, there is always hope.

Mary Frances Bowley

I pray that your heart will be receptive
to what God desires for you.
I pray that you will have the revelation of who Jesus
Christ REALLY is and His love for you.
I pray against any darkness attempting to
distract you from this reality.
I pray for the fullness of God in your life.
There is no greater joy than experiencing the love of
God. There is nothing this world can offer you that
could even compare to our sovereign King.
I pray that you would desire the knowledge of God to
be the foundation of your life. Only in Him can we
live in freedom from the chains of this world.
I pray that the stronghold that has you bowing
to this world will be broken so that you are
able to embrace God in His fullness.
There is NO condemnation in Jesus Christ.
It was Jesus who said, "If any one of you is without
sin, let him be the first to throw a stone at her."

Tracy, one of the Wellspring girls featured in this book,
dedicated this prayer to anyone who is
struggling to see light in his or her life.

Much time and prayer has gone into the crafting of these stories that reveal God's transformational power. We hope that after reading this book, you will be encouraged to pray for the Wellspring girls and consider how you might want to be involved in living dangerously for God.

To find out more about Wellspring Living, Inc. or to make a tax-deductible donation, please check our website:
www.wellspringliving.org.

For more information about Wellspring Living, Inc. curriculum and how to establish a program in your community, call
770-631-8888.

For more information about openings in the Wellspring Home, call
404-427-3100.

Please join us in
Changing Our World by Changing Hers!